New Calvinism is an outstanding collection of essays addressing the phenomenon of a movement that has had a prevailing influence over evangelicalism in the last few decades. This book celebrates the achievements of that movement; recognizes the ways that it has sought to honor the whole counsel of God; while also recognizing the points at which it has compromised with the spirit of the age. It restates the essential elements of the Reformed faith and examines the ways in which those should be recovered and reapplied to the lives of God's people today. It is essential reading.

LIAM GOLIGHER
Senior Minister, Tenth Presbyterian Church, Philadelphia

EDITED BY **JOSH BUICE**

CONTRIBUTORS: **PAUL WASHER, STEVEN J. LAWSON, CONRAD MBEWE,** AND **TIM CHALLIES**

The New Calvinism

CHRISTIAN
FOCUS

Copyright © Josh Buice 2017

paperback ISBN 978-1-5271-0090-9
epub ISBN 978-1-5271-0135-7
mobi ISBN 978-1-5271-0136-4

10 9 8 7 6 5 4 3 2 1

Published in 2017
by
Christian Focus Publications Ltd,
Geanies House, Fearn, Ross-shire,
IV20 1TW, Great Britain.

www.christianfocus.com

Cover design by
Kent Jenson

Printed and bound by
Bell & Bain

CONTENTS

The New Calvinism:

New Reformation or Theological Fad?

❖❖

FIVE centuries ago, Martin Luther nailed his Ninety-Five Theses to the door of the Castle Church in Wittenberg. That single act sparked the Protestant Reformation. Today, the Reformation is not over. The Reformers were protesting against corrupt ideas, false doctrines, and false worship – and those same challenges remain prevalent in our present day and will continue to plague the church of Jesus Christ until our Savior returns.

In recent years, there has been a surge of interest in the doctrines of grace, the Protestant Reformers, and sound biblical theology. In many ways this movement, known by the name *New Calvinism*, is populated by a vast number of younger evangelicals. While we can certainly celebrate a resurgence of sound biblical doctrine in an era that is permeated with shallow pragmatism and spiritual lethargy, we should likewise be concerned by certain deficient methods. One honest question would be, does 'old Calvinism' need to be altered into a movement known as New Calvinism?

What is the *New Calvinism*?

At the heart of the historic Reformation was a true insatiable appetite for God's Word that could not be squelched by fear or flames. Luther made his famous 'Here I stand' response to Rome. Calvin was banished from his pulpit, but when he returned he picked up in the very next verse where he left off. William Tyndale was willing to die at the stake in order to translate and print the English Bible for the common people. These men had an unshakable confidence in the God of the Word, therefore, they labored diligently in the Word of God.

In many ways, the modern resurgence of Calvinism is similar. Today's pastors, in many cases, grew up beneath the cloud or in the wake of controversy in the evangelical world over biblical inerrancy. As a result, their commitment to the Word of God has brought them face-to-face with the doctrines of grace. If the Bible is inerrant and trustworthy, it must be trusted in all verses including John 3:16 and the first two chapters of Ephesians.

In an age of shallow relativism, church marketing pragmatism, and the deep ditches of legalism, a group of people have emerged from the shadows in recent years within the evangelical church who are hungry for God. This group has now been documented as a movement and labeled most recently as the *New Calvinism*. At the heart of New Calvinism is a profound hunger for a God who can address the issues of this fallen world. As this movement looks at the brokenness of drugs, poverty, divorce, and life shattering sins, they see a need for God, and not just a generic god, but specifically the robust sovereign God and ruler of the universe.

In 2008, Collin Hansen went on a journey to document this resurgence. He penned a book titled, *Young, Restless, Reformed: A Journalist's Journey with the New Calvinists*. It caught the attention of many people in the evangelical world and became a focal point as people were trying to assess this new uptick of Calvinistic soteriology. Hansen writes:

> For nearly two years, I traveled across the country and talked with the leading pastors and theologians of the growing Reformed movement. I sat in John Piper's den, Al Mohler's office, C. J. Mahaney's church, and Jonathan Edwards's college. But the backbone of the Reformed resurgence comprises ordinary churches like those I saw in South Dakota – churches used by God to do extraordinary things. Armed with God's Word and transformed by the Holy Spirit, these churches' leaders faithfully proclaim the gospel of Jesus Christ week after week, through tragedy and triumph. Culture has conspired to give their message a wider audience. Desire for transcendence and tradition among young evangelicals has contributed to a Reformed resurgence.[1]

In the following year, *TIME Magazine* ran a series of articles under the banner, '10 Ideas Changing the World Right Now.' Claiming the third spot in this list was 'The New Calvinism.' David Van Biema, in his article, stated the following:

> Calvinism is back, and not just musically. John Calvin's 16th century reply to medieval Catholicism's buy-your-way-out-of-purgatory excesses is Evangelicalism's latest success story, complete with an utterly sovereign and micromanaging deity, sinful and puny humanity, and the combination's logical consequence, predestination: the belief that before time's dawn,

---

1. Collin Hansen, *Young, Restless, and Reformed: A Journalist's Journey with the New Calvinists*, (Wheaton: Crossway Books, 2008), 156.

God decided whom he would save (or not), unaffected by any subsequent human action or decision.[2]

In the United States, it is not entirely uncommon to walk into a coffee shop and see a young bearded man wearing a T-shirt with a picture of Charles Spurgeon in the center of his chest. There seems to be a growing population of younger people who have a love for God and a profound desire to study the Word and think through the deep theological components of the faith. Certainly the numbers indicate that a hunger for sound biblical truth among a certain population within the evangelical world in happening, and it has been building now for a number of years.

A love for theology is not uncommon among young impressionable college students. Although many youthful people populate the New Calvinism, this movement is not reserved for the college campus. Likewise, people in their fifties and sixties are buying reprints in the form of eBooks by Martin Luther and John Calvin on their Kindle and iPad devices. What exactly is happening in the evangelical world? What is New Calvinism? Although difficult to properly define, it's important for us to develop a working definition in order to have a point of reference as we move along through this book.

New Calvinism is a way of describing the youthful movement of people who embrace the rich doctrines of the old Calvinism. Some may argue that it's simply the doctrine of Augustine revived. Others may point beyond Augustine to the apostle Paul. The New Calvinism movement is a broad network that spans across geographic, racial, and denominational boundaries with a high view of God, a profound love for God's Word, a distaste for shallow pragmatism, a commitment to

---

2. David Van Biema, 'The New Calvinism' (TIME Magazine, 2009).

complementarianism, and a true passion for the nations to know Christ. This movement has surged forward in our day through media outlets (that were not present before the Internet) and continue to make their mark through a variety of social networks, blogs, conferences, publishing companies, and vibrant partnerships that span the globe.

Although the New Calvinism movement remains youthful in terms of a movement, the people who make up the movement are not necessarily young. The people of the New Calvinism movement can be defined as an eclectic and at times edgy group of multi-ethnic and age-diverse Reformed people from all parts of the world who are not satisfied with superficial Bible teaching. These people are Christ-exalting, Spirit-driven, missions-motivated, multi-denominational (and non-denominational), charismatic and non-charismatic, and Bible-believing Christians who are seeking to know God, worship God, serve God, and bring glory to God.

At the heart of this movement is an unashamed commitment to the inerrancy of the Bible. Through God's Word, the New Calvinism movement sees everything in life as beneath the providential rule of the transcendent God who is working all things out according to His divine will for His eternal glory.

How Did We Arrive Here?

As always, we find ourselves at this juncture in history under the guidance and providential rule of our sovereign God. We stand upon the shoulders of men like Martin Luther, John Calvin, John Knox, and a host of others who have preached the gospel through the years under the Reformed banner. While this banner may be tattered and bear the marks of doctrinal conflict – the war is not over.

The New Calvinism movement has a certain set of characteristics that are worth noting. A vast number of people today stand connected in a long line of church history. Many Christians today desire to uphold the sufficient Word, defend the faith, and spread the good news of God's grace far and wide. Some notable marks that characterize this modern resurgence of Calvinism include the following:

1. Inerrancy of Scripture
2. Authority of Scripture
3. High view of God
4. Global missions

With a high view of God's Word, a robust view of God's sovereign rule, and an aggressive church planting and missions goal – many modern Calvinists are working across geographic borders and denominational lines in order to accomplish goals for God's glory. In many ways, these newer Calvinists have rediscovered the deep doctrinal wells that the Reformers once upon a time rediscovered from the pages of Scripture. In one sense, the young newer Calvinists are going backward to the old paths.

Certainly we should celebrate this revival of sound doctrine in both the preaching and singing of the gospel. This aggressive resurgence has been noticed, documented, doubted, confirmed, and despised all in recent years. Perhaps all of these different stages have their own merit. However, there is no doubt about it, we have experienced a sudden Calvinistic surge in recent years that is worthy of celebration.

Reasons for Concern

Looking back to the historic Reformation, the hymn writer William Cowper wrote the following:

> At the time of the Reformation the gospel light broke in upon the church. It drove away the clouds of anti-Christian darkness that covered the church. The power of divine grace followed by

the preaching of the Word so that it had visible success in the conversion and building of souls.[3]

One key byproduct of the historic Reformation was the way God changed lives and the way in which people were driven to a pursuit of holiness. It was more than a protest for the sake of visible opposition, instead it was a protest that resulted from a changed heart and an unwavering resolve to stand firm upon God's Word.

All movements, no matter how Christ exalting and biblically accurate, will have variations of opinions and positions. As we examine the modern New Calvinism movement, it's apparent that not everyone is on the same page regarding the meaning of holiness. Some people within the ranks of the New Calvinism movement hold firm to a big God and are passionate about the historic five solas, but they're consistently absent from their local church. They attend coffee shop Bible studies, listen to podcasts, and register for conferences, but they have a lack of zeal for the local church. Many New Calvinists have a lack of desire to submit to pastoral authority and to be used in a stable local church over a long period of successive years. While most New Calvinist pastors and leaders have a healthy view of the local church, there seems to be an anti-institutional vein that runs through this modern movement that doesn't follow in the footsteps of the leaders.

When Christ rules a person's heart, holiness is the by-product. The public behavior that demonstrates a loose tongue along with other immature behavioral characteristics does not display a heart that is under submission. Instead, it appears that many rebellious people cling to their Calvinism, but their gospel is not changing their souls. Where is the devotion to

---

3. R. C. Sproul and Archie Parrish, *The Spirit of Revival – Discovering the Wisdom of Jonathan Edwards*, (Wheaton: Crossway, 2000), 43.

Christ, the love for fellow brethren, the commitment to the local church, and the desire for personal holiness? These characteristics are not true of New Calvinism alone, they are found in all branches of evangelicalism in our day. For New Calvinism however, the contradiction arises out of the big God approach to life that clashes with loose living among some of the immature people who make up the New Calvinism movement.

Many people within the New Calvinism movement would find the piety of the historic Reformation to be profitable. Unfortunately, not everyone who identifies with this movement would seem to agree. With certain voices promoting a lack of holiness under the name of Christian freedom, their fall into immorality has not come as a massive surprise. In some ways, these falling stars are almost expected, although it hinders the entire movement and discredits the deep doctrine that serves as the foundation for the New Calvinism.

In explaining the historic Reformation, John MacArthur writes:

> The Reformation was the inevitable and explosive consequence of the Word of God crashing like a massive tidal wave against the thin barricades of man-made tradition and hypocritical religion. As the common people of Europe gained access to the Scriptures in their own language, the Spirit of God used that timeless truth to convict their hearts and convert their souls. The result was utterly transformative, not only for the lives of individual sinners, but for the entire continent on which they resided.[4]

Instead of asking if the New Calvinism is a legitimate movement, the question today is framed in this way: *will the New*

---

4. John MacArthur, *Strange Fire: The Danger of Offending the Holy Spirit with Counterfeit Worship*, (Nashville: Nelson Books, 2013), 213.

Calvinism last? The jury remains out on this question and only decades of time will properly answer this question.

The purpose of this book is to compliment and critique the New Calvinism movement. While I happily identify with the New Calvinism on many levels, there are certain aspects of the movement that need to be addressed. What you will read in this book will touch on many of the dangers that lurk in the shadows – and at times seem to arise at the center of the movement. These dangers must not be ignored.

The first chapter will be focused on sola Scriptura and the battleground of the sufficiency of Scripture over against religious pragmatism. The second chapter will be centered on the doctrine of ecclesiology and will explain why the New Calvinism movement will not survive without a robust commitment to the local church. Chapter three will explain why a passionate pursuit of holiness is key to the health of the New Calvinism movement – or any God centered movement for that matter. In the fourth chapter the focus will be on the need for the Spirit of God to empower his people for the work of ministry and Christian living. Finally, in the fifth chapter, there will be a call to biblical discernment. Our enemy is crafty and he will place traps before us in various forms that could damage our individual testimony for Christ and derail the New Calvinism movement.

1

Sola Scriptura – Is the Bible Enough?

Josh Buice

JUST before Christmas in 2014, an article appeared in *Newsweek* magazine that stated the following:

> No television preacher has ever read the Bible. Neither has any evangelical politician. Neither has the pope. Neither have I. And neither have you. At best, we've all read a bad translation – a translation of translations of translations of hand-copied copies of copies of copies of copies, and on and on, hundreds of times.[1]

That statement by Kurt Eichenwald may not seem earth shaking, but it's proof that the battle over the Bible is not finished. When my eyes caught that article sitting on the

---

1. Kurt Eichenwald, 'The Bible: So Misunderstood It's a Sin' (*Newsweek*, December 23, 2014).

shelf in a store across the street from my church campus, it was a reminder that many people still hate the Bible and reject its authority. The attack on the Word of God started in the Garden of Eden and now it appears on a shelf at a local Dollar Store just west of Atlanta. This attack is not reserved for the intellectual elites – and it continues to be rehashed in varied settings from seminary classrooms to obscure YouTube channels.

It was Martin Luther, on October 31, 1517, who protested against the Roman Catholic Church and the abuse of indulgences by nailing his Ninety-Five Theses to the door of the Castle Church in Wittenberg. Nobody, including the Augustinian monk himself, would have predicted the explosion of controversy that erupted after the protest was made public.

Martin Luther (1483–1546) would rise to the forefront of this movement that has become known as the Protestant Reformation. At the core of this movement was a commitment to God's Word. The Reformation was not about Calvinism. The Reformation was about the recovery of the authority and the sufficiency of Scripture. As a direct result, the Reformation had a profound impact upon the pulpit as men stood and proclaimed the Word of God boldly. This in turn, had a lasting impact upon the church as a whole.

The battle cry of the Protestant Reformation was *sola Scriptura*. Out of the Reformation era came five definitive doctrinal positions that categorize the convictions of those men and women who risked much, and in some cases, gave everything to defend the faith once delivered to the saints. These Latin slogans are:

+ *Sola Fide* – by faith alone.
+ *Sola Scriptura* – Scripture alone.

+ *Solus Christus* – through Christ alone.
+ *Sola Gratia* – by grace alone.
+ *Soli Deo Gloria* – glory to God alone.

The foundation whereby these statements stand or fall is *sola Scriptura*. If the Scriptures are not trustworthy, how can we know the truth of our human depravity, the glory of Jesus' substitutionary death, and the amazing grace of God granted to depraved sinners?

For many years, the Roman Catholic Church had a stranglehold on the Bible. They wanted to control the Bible by adding to it their traditions and subjugating the authority of the Bible by the authority of the magisterium. The issue of authority was at the heart of the protest of the Reformation. Once upon a time, the Roman Catholic Church was willing to burn people at the stake to maintain control of the Bible. Likewise it must be emphasized, once upon a time Christians were willing to endure the hot flames of persecution in order to preach and publish the Bible in the common man's language. Where are such men today?

Modern *Fad* or Real *Resurgence?*

Is the New Calvinism movement a real resurgence, a genuine movement, a modern reformation, or merely a theological fad? Although it's largely considered a movement, the overall successes and failures remain to be seen at this point. Although there is much reason to rejoice, we must not celebrate prematurely. It will take a while for enough water to flow beneath the bridge before we can chart the successes or failures of this movement in totality. However, there is something to be said of New Calvinism for the great number of young evangelicals who are hungry for biblical truth.

Where did all of these *new* Calvinists come from? It's no secret that it has become cool to be a Calvinist, and some have been swayed over by cultural additives rather than biblical truth. Today, long beards, trendy tattoos, and hipster attire are being added to the old Calvinistic theology. While many younger people are reading the theologians of old as they form their understanding of God's work in salvation – is this movement growing based on the depth of theology or the cultural winds?

When people are willing to take long road trips or fly across the ocean to gather for a weekend conference on discipleship, we must all agree that this is not a normal thing within church history. The resurgence of sound doctrine must ultimately be attributed to God. The rise in theological hunger is based on God using local churches, conferences, blogs, books, songs, technology, and most importantly – the Holy Spirit to accomplish His purpose.

If you look at the way technology has developed in recent years, it must be noted that the technological boom and the modern resurgence of Calvinism are closely connected. With a few clicks of a button, the works of Luther, Calvin, Edwards, Knox, Warfield, Spurgeon, and other notable figures from church history can be accessed on an electronic device – including a smart phone. Within this technological boom, daily articles are published on blog sites where pastors, theologians, scholars, and authors are connecting with multitudes of people. With the use of social media platforms, the connections become more efficient and the audience interaction becomes more specific. There never has been a time in history where information was as easily attainable as it is today.

Another way in which New Calvinism continues to gain strength is through theologically rich songs that have doctrinal depth. Years ago, the church was led to sing songs full of rich theology about a sovereign God who rules the universe and saves sinners. In modern times, the singing of the church was hijacked by song writers who produced songs that were theologically anemic and lacking in substance.

Within this resurgence of Reformed theology, the church has been reintroduced to lyrics that are saturated with deep theological truths. These new Reformed lyrics show up on screens in worship services, in newly organized hymnals, and on radio stations to audiences that transcend the local church gathering. There has also been a resurgence of interest in the old theologically rich hymns from church history. Rather than turning off the younger generation, multitudes of young Christians have grown to embrace songs of praise that are full of sound biblical truth through modern hymn writers like Keith and Kristyn Getty and Sovereign Grace Music.

There is more to being Reformed than reading certain blogs and dressing in T-shirts containing the faces of Luther, Calvin, Edwards, Knox, and Spurgeon. What about the Word of God? Is the Bible being handled with humility and preached with authority? If the Reformation was sparked by a passionate commitment to the authority of the Bible, where does the authority of the Bible fit into this New Calvinism movement?

In this chapter, I would like to provide an encouragement and sound a warning to the New Calvinism movement regarding the Reformation principle of *sola Scriptura*. While many of the New Calvinist pastors and church members are nowhere near the line of danger – some are walking a fine line of compromise in our day. The world has witnessed too many falling stars already. Any step in the direction of pragmatism is a step in the wrong direction.

The Fuel of the Reformation

The fuel of the historic Reformation was centered on a passion for the Scriptures. The Roman Catholic Church had silenced the pulpits. What flowed out of the Reformation was a commitment to the veracity and reliability of God's Word. During the Reformation, people gave their lives in order for us to hold a modern translation of the Bible in our hands and hear it preached from the pulpit. During the early days of the Protestant Reformation, a commitment to the Scriptures was a dangerous thing – one that could cost a man his life.

As we look back over the history of the evangelical church, we observe times of great health and times of great decline. In modern times, seasons of decline can be traced to days where conservative men stood in the pulpit and talked about the importance of being conservative and talked about the Word of God but didn't actually preach the Word of God. Moralism won the day, and that's why Christian Smith, a sociologist at Notre Dame, in his book from 2005, *Soul Searching: The Religious and Spiritual Lives of American Teenagers*, coined the term 'moralistic therapeutic deism' as he described the predominant religious position of teenagers in America.

According to Smith, the common faith of teenagers across the board can be summarized in the belief that God's goal for our lives is for us to be happy. Smith notes that although most students acknowledge that God exists, He isn't involved intimately with His creation – according to their way of thinking. According to Smith's research, the prevailing religious thought among young people on the college campus is that God wants us to be good to others, and this behavior is anchored deep in the mire of moralism rather than the pure gospel of Christ.

One primary reason for the success of the New Calvinism movement is based upon a desire to hear God speak in intimate and prophetic ways to this world from the pages of the Bible. The New Calvinism resurgence is populated by a large number of people who are hungry for truth and look to the Word of God as the single authoritative source for truth.

This is something that we should celebrate and emphasize within our local churches.

When we see women hungering for God's Word and spending time reading serious theological books with other ladies in their church, this should encourage us. When we see men with grease under their fingernails reading the Bible on lunch break and daily blog articles at night to sharpen their theological muscle – we should be encouraged. When teenagers are found engaging in social media conversations over the Word of God and sound biblical theology, this should excite us. When college students have a hunger for robust expository preaching, this should ignite our hearts with much encouragement. But we must proceed with caution.

The same movement that was sparked by a hunger for God through His Word can be derailed by pragmatism, mysticism, and many other false ideas that are lingering on the periphery awaiting an opportunity to strike. Not only will the church become weak, superficial, pragmatic, legalistic, and lifeless, but the overall movement will die a young death if the Word of God is deemphasized. If bold expository preaching gives way to drama teams and musical performances, it will be disastrous to the Reformed resurgence. The life of the church is directly connected to her commitment to holy Scripture. Children taught theology-lite today will not withstand the attack of enemies such as Bart Ehrman tomorrow.[2] Doctrine matters, and sound biblical theology must be the emphasis from the church's pulpit on a weekly basis.

---

2. Bart Ehrman is an agnostic New Testament scholar and Professor of Religious Studies at the University of North Carolina at Chapel Hill. He is considered to be one of the top scholarly opponents to biblical inerrancy and sufficiency.

Avoiding the Dangers of Pragmatism and Cultural Relevance

As we consider the New Calvinism movement, we must celebrate the recovery of sound biblical doctrines that have been the outflow of an emphasis upon the inerrancy and authority of the Bible. Unfortunately, there are some deficiencies that must be addressed. If the New Calvinism movement will continue to march forward, more reformation must take place within the evangelical church.

We must face the issue of biblical authority and sufficiency. Many Reformed Christians claim to be people of the Book, but is that completely true? What would Calvin say to the present day young Reformed man who is sitting at Starbucks on Sunday rather than being immersed into a local church? Are the Scriptures authoritative? Is submission to the authority of the Bible necessary? Why are so many people who claim to embrace sound theology resistant to leaders in the local church?

While many Reformed people are not likely to be found entrapped by heavenly tourism books such as *Heaven Is For Real*, there is a real danger when it comes to pragmatic church growth strategies and discipleship methods. Why is the pragmatism trap so dangerous even among the New Calvinism movement? Perhaps at the heart of pragmatic methodology is the fact that nobody wants to be viewed as a failure. Success is a drug that entices Christians across the evangelical spectrum. The god of church growth and the idol of 'bigness' have a way of enticing people and equipping them with necessary tools to reach their pragmatic goals. These goals, however, almost always come at the expense of sound theology and church health.

We may not be living in 1954 when the Southern Baptist Convention promoted a campaign of church growth under the banner, 'A Million More in '54,' but the church has become extremely focused on packaging ministries into a neatly wrapped gift to the community rather than remaining focused on the exposition and explanation of Scripture. Should the weekly worship service be tailored for the unbelieving community around the church campus or should it be structured for the church to gather and worship God?

Long before the church worries about the peripheral issues of ministry packaging, we must put a heavy concentration upon the exposition and application of the Bible. People need to hear from God before they are overwhelmed with the appearance of our signage, how modern our stage sets are arranged, or how advanced our technology team has become.

While many people within the New Calvinism movement remain vocally opposed to the deep ruts of pragmatism, why do a number of New Calvinist pastors seem to have a heavy focus on their stage set design, cultural attire, and cultural engagements as a means of *reaching* the culture?

It may be a response to legalism that causes many church leaders to head off down the broken road of pragmatism – but that is not a valid excuse. This type of thinking has affected everything from the preaching delivery to the pastor's attire. The pendulum of yesterday's legalism has swung in the direction of the golden rule of pragmatism which says, 'If it works – do it.'

In many cases, it doesn't stop with attire and trendy sermon delivery. People continue to push the limits while boasting of their Christian freedoms. Even within the New Calvinism movement, people are suggesting that they're reaching a group of people as a result of their trendiness that otherwise would never be reached by the average conservative church ministry. Is this assumption valid? Does this pragmatic rule deny the doctrine of God's sovereignty and the sufficiency of Scripture?

The assumption that casual attire and edgy Christian liberty will attract a group of people that would not likely attend a *regular* or more *traditional* church setting may actually be correct. The real question is – what are such churches reaching the culture with? Are they attracting people by their music, technology, stage, and relevant tattoo art – or is it the gospel of Jesus Christ? It must be emphasized – what you use to win people with is what you must use to keep people happy. This is where pragmatism and a lack of biblical depth often becomes a much more attractive and successful model of church growth than a model built primarily upon the Scriptures.

Our modern evangelical church culture is swimming in a cesspool of pragmatic trickery. The primacy of preaching has been replaced with church growth trends. Such gimmicks reveal shame for the gospel of Jesus and His bloody cross. This modern fascination with the god of 'bigness' causes pastors and church leaders to capitulate on the absolute sufficiency of Scripture. While this is not the case with every church, it is the common practice of our day. Steven Lawson, in his book *Famine in the Land*, documents this error by writing:

> A new way of 'doing' church is emerging. In this radical paradigm shift, exposition is being replaced with entertainment, preaching with performances, doctrine with drama, and theology with theatrics. The pulpit, once the focal point of the church, is now being overshadowed by a variety of church-growth techniques, everything from trendy worship styles to glitzy presentations and vaudeville-like pageantries. In seeking to capture the upper hand in church growth, a new wave of pastors is reinventing church and repackaging the gospel into a product to be sold to 'consumers.'[3]

---

3. Steven J. Lawson, *Famine in the Land* (Chicago: Moody Publishers, 2003), 25.

The need of the hour is not ecclesiastical entrepreneurs or marketing strategists to lead the church onward. The ultimate honor of success is not the status of 'relevant' or 'hipster' church. Be sure that these labels and trends will die soon and be replaced with other categories. Although a great number of people among the New Calvinism movement stand opposed to such religious trickery, the temptation to use such methods for fast results is consistently present. While many people argue that the age of pragmatism has passed, we continue to see the fruit of such models prevalent in the edgy trends of the New Calvinism movement.

What has Christ commissioned us to do? He has sent us out to preach the Word and make disciples. While we can use new methods such as smart phone applications, social media platforms, and blog sites – at the same time we must rest in the power of the gospel to save sinners and bring people out of darkness and into the marvelous light of Christ.

If people are attracted to the New Calvinism movement because of cultural additives or an edgy appearance – do they really understand Calvinism? Historic Calvinism was not about an edgy cultural appearance or a rogue religious attitude – it was about the gospel. At its foundation, the New Calvinism was not born for that purpose either. For New Calvinism to be a lasting reformation – any attempt to move in that direction must be avoided.

The world will never think the gospel is cool. If the New Calvinism movement is indeed a new reformation, the people who make up this movement must stop accommodating their culture and boldly preach the Scriptures. The gospel will never be palatable to depraved sinners apart from a spiritual resurrection performed by God. As we study the work of God in conversion, we must admit that the church's cultural trends are not what brought a person to a saving knowledge of the gospel.

Salvation is of the Lord. If you're known for something other than the gospel of Jesus – something has gone awry. Remember, when people walked for miles to find Adoniram Judson, they were asking everyone where the 'Jesus Christ' man was so that they could hear and obtain the good news from the Scriptures. They were not being attracted to him because of his choice of cultural additives. In chapter 10 and paragraph 2 of the 1689 London Baptist Confession of Faith, we find these words on effectual calling:

> This effectual call flows from God's free and special grace alone, not from anything at all foreseen in those called. Neither does the call arise from any power or action on their part; they are totally passive in it. They are dead in sins and trespasses until they are made alive and renewed by the Holy Spirit. By this they are enabled to answer this call and to embrace the grace offered and conveyed in it. This response is enabled by a power that is no less than that which raised Christ from the dead.

It should be noted that God calls sinners to Himself by grace through the Holy Spirit who brings about a response to the gospel. This is a work of God – and not one trend or gimmick will share in God's glory of saving sinners.

The Crisis of Confidence in God's Word

The liberal agenda continues to sway people away from the Bible as they attempt to replace it with other sources – defective and deficient substitutes that echo the voices of everyone other than God. While many in the New Calvinism movement abhor that type of agenda, any movement away from *sola Scriptura* toward other methods to 'grow' churches is a tragic mistake. The New Calvinists do have a high view of Scripture, but there is a need to help many of these young believers see how the Scripture that they believe should be embraced as the authoritative revelation of God that governs their faith and practice.

When the apostle Paul was preparing Timothy for pastoral ministry in the city of Ephesus, he wrote the following words:

> All Scripture is breathed out by God and profitable for teaching, for reproof, for correction, and for training in righteousness, that the man of God may be complete, equipped for every good work (2 Tim. 3:16-17 ESV).

Before getting to the classic pinnacle of Paul's letter in 2 Timothy 4:1-5 where Paul emphatically called upon Timothy to 'preach the Word,' he began with a clear statement regarding Scripture's source and sufficiency. Regarding the source of Scripture, Paul said that 'all Scripture' is 'breathed out by God.' The phrase, 'breathed out by God' is one word in the original Greek text – θεόπνευστος. This particular word literally means that all Scripture comes from *the breath of God*. Since God is the source of the Scriptures, the Scriptures are authoritative and cannot be replaced by any other book, resource, or substitute.

It should likewise be noted that Paul instructed Timothy regarding the sufficiency of Scripture. Ephesus was a city saturated with sin. The city of Ephesus was located on the coastal region of modern day Turkey. It had four main roads that intersected in the midst of the city causing it to gain the nickname, 'gateway to Asia.' The ancient city of Ephesus has been labeled the 'Vanity Fair' of the ancient world.

As a progressive city, Ephesus boasted of trade, athletic competitions, and the temple of Artemis (the false goddess known as Diana). Interestingly enough, Paul didn't instruct Timothy to contextualize his gospel into the popular religion practiced in Ephesus. Paul likewise didn't instruct Timothy to perform drama presentations in the great theater in order to slip in the gospel through a backdoor approach. Timothy wasn't instructed on his cultural attire or stage design in order to gain relevance. Paul instructed Timothy to preach the gospel in the context of an urbane people who loved their sin.

While the entire New Calvinist movement would be diametrically opposed to the doctrine and methods of Rob Bell, even the pastors within the New Calvinism camp are not immune to the cultural downgrade and attack upon the preaching of God's Word. It's not cool to be a preacher of the gospel, and many pastors have lost confidence as a preacher of righteousness. We must not forget that Noah was not cool and popular among the culture of his day.

In an age where men are avoiding the title of *preacher* in exchange for Christian communicator, conference speaker, life coach, blogger, and other fancy titles – it's helpful to see that Paul was directing Timothy to *preach* the Word (2 Tim. 4:1-5). The office of preacher is not a shameful office, it's a biblical office that God has ordained. To be ashamed of the calling to preach the Bible is to be ashamed of God. We are called to represent God rather than pursuing relevance and cultural popularity.

There is a crisis of confidence in God's Word in our modern evangelical era, and the New Calvinism movement is not immune to this problem. Although many pastors in the New Calvinism movement faithfully preach the Word, there are still too many sermonettes being given each Lord's Day – even among professing reformed preachers. There are still many *talkers* who need to be transformed into *preachers*.

When pragmatism overshadows theology, the end result will be compromise. The need of the hour is for our orthopraxy to match our orthodoxy. When pastors capitulate on *sola Scriptura*, the entire church suffers. This methodological shift will affect everyone from the children to the senior adults. We are guilty of creating functional atheism when we distance ourselves from the authority and reliability of God's Word.

New Calvinists are not being confused with theological liberals by any stretch, but the cultural pressures to lighten up and avoid taking the Bible too seriously are perpetually present – even among the New Calvinism movement. All true preachers of God's Word feel a certain pressure to avoid being too *preachy*.

Meanwhile, liberals are awaiting children from evangelical churches, and with open arms they receive a new crop of them onto the university campuses each fall. Once these students are isolated from their homes and their local churches, professors go on immediate attack against the authority of God's Word. Much like Satan in the Garden of Eden, they arrogantly cast doubt upon the reliability of God's Word. One such professor is Harvey Cox, a man who has been teaching at Harvard Divinity school for over fifty years. In his recent book titled, *How To Read The Bible*, Cox writes:

> In view of this historically informed reading of Paul [Rom. 1:26-27], more and more churches today are placing a 'welcoming and affirming' sign on their doors. And in those churches (as in the one I attend) gay and lesbian people bring their children to morning worship and Sunday school, sing in the choirs, take up the collection, and more and more frequently stand in the pulpit. Most long for just what everyone else wants:

respect, appreciation, and loving long-term relationships, including marriage. Even Pope Francis declares that he is not in a position to judge them. Yet in many churches these people still sometimes hear the words from Paul thrown at them like fiery darts. But I think this ugly chapter in Christian history is ending, and those dart throwers will be remembered solely the way we remember those tiresome opponents of abolition and racial justice who in times past marshaled isolated verses to support their cause.[4]

Classic liberals and modern skeptics continue to attack the authority and reliability of the Bible. As they continue to chip away at the Bible, conservative minds are left to question the sufficiency of Scripture for a modern audience. Is the Bible enough or do we need a revised edition for our modern culture? Sinclair Ferguson writes, 'He [God] reveals himself in its [the Bible] pages, speaks in its sentences and does so in order to bring us to trust, know, and love him.'[5]

Today's church culture is enamored with sophistication, modern advancements, and an array of modern techniques for ministry. This often causes the emphasis of the local church to be placed on everything other than the Bible. The New Calvinism movement is not insulated from this danger. Charles Spurgeon, in a sermon titled, 'How to Read the Bible,' said the following, 'How little of Scripture there is in modern sermons compared with the sermons of those masters of theology, the Puritanic divines!'[6] When students

---

4. Harvey Cox, *How To Read The Bible*, (New York: HarperCollins, 2015), 184.

5. Sinclair Ferguson, *From The Mouth of God*, (Edinburgh: The Banner of Truth Trust, 2014), 4.

6. C. H. Spurgeon, *The Metropolitan Tabernacle Pulpit Sermons*, vol. 25 (London: Passmore & Alabaster, 1879), 626.

leave your church for the university, they need to remember the doctrines preached from the Scriptures more than the fancy stage lighting that you have in your sanctuary. Make no mistake, doctrine matters.

Consider the account of King Herod's confusion regarding the identity of Jesus. In Mark 6:14-29, the popularity of Jesus was brought to Herod's attention and he insisted that Jesus was John the Baptist raised from the dead. Herod's options regarding Jesus' identity included John the Baptist, Elijah, or one of the prophets of old. Herod chose John the Baptist.

If we examine the preaching ministry of the Baptist, we see that he was not ashamed to preach the Word of God and point people to repentance. The same is true of Elijah who triumphed in victory over the prophets of Baal. The prophets were known as resolute and strong preachers who were unwilling to compromise. One look at Samuel and the whole scene with King Agag (1 Sam. 15) proves this to be true. All of these men were preachers with conviction, and Jesus was mistaken as one of those men. Such a misidentification communicates much truth about Jesus' preaching ministry. Couple that with Jesus' commitment to the reliability of God's Word (see Matt. 4:4; 12:40; 19:4-5; Luke 20:37), and it's evident that Jesus was a preacher who not only believed the Word of God – but He likewise proclaimed it.

The need of this hour is for faithful men to embrace the office of preacher and receive the mantle of preaching with glad and courageous hearts. The health of the church is always connected to the health of the pulpit. If men who stand in the pulpit are ashamed to *preach the Word*, their disciples will likewise learn to be ashamed of the gospel of Jesus Christ. John Calvin once defined preaching as 'the living voice' of God 'in His church.'[7] He went on to explain, 'It is by the preaching of the grace of God alone that the church is kept from perishing.'[8]

A Return to *Sola Scriptura*

As I've argued earlier in this chapter, some of the people who make up the New Calvinism movement need to return to a firm commitment to God's Word. Even the slightest slip in this area will lead to further capitulation, and compromise always leads to theological liberalism. Some of the problems articulated in this chapter related to mainstream evangelicalism have started to appear in the New Calvinism movement – including cultural pragmatism. A firm commitment to God's Word is the only way to prevent a Bible loving people from theological disaster.

Looking at the evangelical church in his day, James Montgomery Boice said, 'Inerrancy is not the most critical issue facing the church today. The most serious issue, I believe, is the Bible's sufficiency.'[9] Therefore, the New Calvinism movement was birthed in a time when churches and church leaders were rethinking the sufficiency of Scripture. That same debate continues to rage today. To allow any deviation from the firm foundation of *sola Scriptura* is to deny the absolute sufficiency of God's Word. If God has spoken, His Word is enough. The true test of the New Calvinism will be evident as new pressures and

---

7. John Calvin, *Commentaries on the Four Last Books of Moses Arranged in the Form of a Harmony*, trans. Charles William Bingham (Grand Rapids, MI: Baker Books, 1979 reprint), 235.

8. John Calvin, *Commentary on the Book of Psalms*, vol. 1, trans. James Anderson (Grand Rapids, MI: Baker Books, 1979 reprint), 388-89.

9. James Montgomery Boice, *Whatever Happened to the Gospel of Grace?* (Wheaton: Crossway, 2001), 72.

temptations are paraded before the eyes of this movement. Will something attract the New Calvinism movement to capitulate on *sola Scriptura*?

Today's contemporary Christian has the privilege of using an array of modern technological and media advancements. In like manner, today's church assembles in advanced church buildings designed for efficient meeting space equipped with state of the art technology to aid in discipleship. Although the church enjoys the modern advancements of technology – the primitive methods of preaching and the centrality of preaching in the life of the church must not be abandoned.

Standing Upon the Shoulders of Faithful Men

Consider the men who have shaped us from history. We owe a great deal of debt to those men who have stood valiantly and courageously to defend the inerrancy and sufficiency of God's Word – and some of those voices are leaders in the New Calvinism movement such as John Piper and D. A. Carson. May our Lord be pleased to raise up other men to do the exact same thing in our age of pluralism and secular thinking. What if the New Calvinism movement looked back in history to such unflinching examples of Christian fortitude and gospel ministry as the Reformers and the Puritans? May the Lord use these examples to reinvigorate a passionate and resolute confidence in God's Word.

MARTIN LUTHER: We stand upon the shoulders of Martin Luther (1483–1546). As Steven Lawson has rightly stated, 'As Martin Luther took his bold stance, whether in the pulpit or before cardinals and councils, he was firmly anchored to the impregnable rock of Scripture.'[10] As Luther labored in

---

10. Steven Lawson, *The Heroic Boldness of Martin Luther*, (Sanford, FL:

his writing and preaching, he viewed the pulpit as the throne of God.[11] From his Ninety-Five Theses to his relentless preaching, Luther stood courageously upon the sacred Scriptures.

For Luther, his foundation for ministry was built upon the steady and sure rock of the Bible. In a day when the Roman Catholic Church had locked the Bible in a dark dungeon, Luther labored tirelessly to open the dungeon and release the light of Scriptures upon the parched souls of starving people. Luther's ministry can be summarized by a line from his hymn, 'A Mighty Fortress,' which states:

> Let goods and kindred go, this mortal life also;
> The body they may kill: God's truth abideth still,
> His kingdom is forever.

Martin Luther had an unwavering commitment to God's Word. Fred Meuser observes, 'In 1522 he preached 117 sermons in Wittenberg and 137 sermons the next year. In 1528 he preached almost 200 times, and from 1529 we have 121 sermons. So the average in those four years was one sermon every two-and-a-half days.'[12] In order for the trajectory of the New Calvinism movement to move forward with health and strength, the preachers must labor in the Scriptures with the assurance that the enemies of God will never be able to kill the truth of God's Word.

JOHN CALVIN: We stand upon the shoulders of John Calvin (1509–1564). It was Calvin who immersed himself

---

Reformation Trust, 2013), 61 (epub edition).

11. Martin Luther, cited in *More Gathered Gold: A Treasury of Quotataions for Christians*, comp. John Blanchard (Hertfordshire, England: Evangelical Press, 1986), 243.

12. Fred W. Meuser, *Luther the Preacher* (Minneapolis: Augsburg Publishing House, 1983), 37-38.

into God's Word like a well of pure and living water. John Calvin said, 'The Majesty of Scripture deserves that its expounders should make it apparent, that they proceed to handle it with modesty and reverence.'[13] This high regard for the authority of Scripture shaped all of Calvin's life and ministry. If the New Calvinism movement will be true to the name of Calvin, there must be a firm commitment to *sola Scriptura*. Calvin stated, 'We owe to the Scripture the same reverence which we owe to God because it has proceeded from Him alone, and has nothing of man mixed with it.'[14] Theodore Beza, commenting on John Calvin, stated, '*Tot verba, tot pondera*, "every word weighed a pound".'[15] There was a seriousness to Calvin's approach to the pulpit, and we desperately need men today who feel the weight of the preacher's mantle.

JOHN KNOX: We stand upon the shoulders of the Father of the Scottish Reformation – John Knox (1514–1572). Certainly one of the towering figures of the Reformation and of church history as a whole, this courageous preacher stood up in the face of adversity and labored for more than his church or his city – he labored for all of Scotland. The landscape of Scotland was overrun with superstition and popish babble, the Bible was closed, and the gospel was veiled behind the false system of the Roman Catholic Church's works-based false salvation. Steven Lawson describes Knox by writing 'If

---

13. John Calvin, *Commentary on a Harmony of the Evangelists, Matthew, Mark, and Luke*, vol. 1, trans. William Pringle (Grand Rapids, MI: Baker Books, 1979 reprint), 227.

14. John Calvin, as quoted in J. I. Packer, 'Calvin the Theologian,' in *John Calvin: A Collection of Essays*, ed. James Atkinson, et al. (Grand Rapids, MI: Eerdmans Publishing Co., 1966), 166.

15. John Albert Broadus, *Lectures on the History of Preaching* (New York: Sheldon & Company, 1876), 120.

Martin Luther was the hammer of the Reformation and John Calvin the pen, John Knox was the trumpet.'[16]

Although he is buried beneath parking place number 23 behind St Giles Cathedral and often overlooked in Edinburgh, his voice still echoes across the landscape of Scotland. Some men are visionaries and zealous in their approach to ministry, and that can certainly be said of Knox as he built his entire ministry on the mission statement: 'Give me Scotland, or I die.' A staunchly Reformed preacher and anti-Catholic, Knox would devote his life to the Reformation of Scotland and beyond. Mary Queen of Scots went on record in 1561 as stating that John Knox was the most dangerous man in her Kingdom. Burk Parsons writes:

> He reinvigorated God's shepherds throughout the nation; this, in turn, reformed the church and, thus, in God's providence, revived the country. Most notably, what inspired the pastors perhaps more than any other characteristic in Knox was that he did not fear men, because he feared God – he was a man willing to offend men, because he was unwilling to offend God.[17]

GEORGE WHITEFIELD: We stand upon the shoulders of George Whitefield (1714–1770) who placed the Scriptures at the forefront of his ministry. When we think of Whitefield preaching in the open-air, we think of his fiery passion and thundering voice. The fuel of Whitefield's passion was the Word of God. He lived in a day where men were more consumed with the writings of secular poets, philosophers,

---

16. Steven Lawson, *John Knox: Fearless Faith* (Scotland: Christian Focus, 2017), 15.

17. Burk Parsons, 'Give Me Scotland, or I Die' (Tabletalk, March 1, 2014).

and rhetoricians, but Whitefield's love was the Bible. It was the pattern of Whitefield in his study to read the text of Scripture and then pray over '"every line and every word" in both the English and Greek, feasting his mind and his heart upon it till its essential meaning became a part of his very person.'[18]

Whitefield was respected by Charles Spurgeon as 'the chief of preachers.' The soul of Whitefield became a furnace where the Scriptures burned hot within the eighteenth century preacher. He preached 18,000 sermons in his preaching career. If you add to his sermons the meditations and other addresses, he preached over 30,000 sermons. That was 1,000 times per year for thirty straight years. The need of our present hour is for men to be consumed with the Scriptures like George Whitefield. For when the pulpit is set on fire by the Word of God, the blaze will spread throughout the entire church. If the New Calvinism movement will move onward, the pastors and church leaders must major on preaching. We need more biblical preaching – not less.

JOHN BUNYAN: We stand upon the shoulders of a tinker named John Bunyan (1628–1688), a pastor in Bedford, England during the seventeenth century. Bunyan was saturated with God's Word. While in jail for preaching the gospel, he penned the most printed book in world history other than the Bible, titled, *The Pilgrim's Progress.* Charles Spurgeon read *The Pilgrim's Progress* at least once per year because it was laced with God's Word. Spurgeon said of Bunyan, 'Why, this man is a living Bible! Prick him anywhere; and you will find that his blood is Bibline; the very essence of the Bible

---

18. Arnold Dallimore, *George Whitefield: The Life and Times of the Great Evangelist of the 18ᵗʰ Century Revival*, vol. 1 (1970, repr.; Edinburgh: Banner of Truth, 1995), 268.

flows from him. He cannot speak without quoting a text, for his soul is full of the Word of God.'[19]

Why was Bunyan imprisoned? It was for preaching the Word of God. He could have walked out of the jail in Bedford if he would have agreed to remain silent and stop preaching the Scriptures. That was not an option for Bunyan, so he remained in jail for twelve years while his children grew and his wife labored to care for them. His resolute confidence rested upon the Scriptures. Where are such men today? If the New Calvinism movement will become healthy, it must be led on by men with such confidence in God's Word.

JONATHAN EDWARDS: We stand upon the shoulders of Jonathan Edwards (1703–1758). Many people believe that Edwards was one of the most brilliant thinkers in American history. He was used by God in the period of the Great Awakening. As a pastor, he was a theologian who stood in the sacred desk of God without blushing as he proclaimed the truths of Scripture. Known for his passion for the lost as he preached his famous sermon titled, 'Sinners in the Hands of an Angry God' – he zealously pointed people to repent and call upon the name of the Lord for salvation.

While at Yale, Edwards penned a list of resolutions. The twenty-eighth resolution stated, 'Resolved: To study the Scriptures so steadily, constantly, and frequently, as that I may find, and plainly perceive, myself to grow in the knowledge of the same.' Edwards had a passion for God's Word and it was his time spent in the Word that kindled the flame in his soul to proclaim the Word faithfully. His preaching exemplified the reality that he had spent time with God through His Word. As Conrad Mbewe rightly stated,

---

19. Charles Spurgeon, *Autobiography* (Edinburgh: Banner of Truth, 1973), 2:159.

'The reason that so many pastors have abandoned the Bible for a perennial diet of jokes and anecdotes is that they have not been cultivating their gift of biblical exposition. In short, they do not know how to use the Bible properly.'[20]

CHARLES HADDON SPURGEON: We stand upon the shoulders of Charles Spurgeon (1834–1892). Spurgeon was a man who refused to embrace any other tactic outside of Scripture for the foundation of success in his ministry. Spurgeon preached the sacred Scriptures in an age of evangelical downgrade in England. When other pulpits were merely echoing the ideas and philosophies of man, Spurgeon thundered the Word of God. Spurgeon once said:

> These words are God's. ... Thou book of vast authority, thou art a proclamation from the Emperor of Heaven; far be it from me to exercise my reason in contradicting thee. ... This is the book untainted by any error; but it is pure unalloyed, perfect truth. Why? Because God wrote it.[21]

It was not by accident that 25,000 copies of Spurgeon's sermons sold each week in twenty different languages. Spurgeon, with conviction, preached the Bible without shame. When Spurgeon approached the pulpit, it was guaranteed that the source of Spurgeon's sermon was the Bible. For Spurgeon, nothing else would do. He had an unashamed confidence in the Word of God.

DAVID MARTYN LLOYD-JONES: We stand upon the shoulders of a medical doctor who became a faithful expositor of God's Word named D. Martyn Lloyd-Jones (1899–1981).

---

20. Conrad Mbewe, *Foundations For The Flock*, (Hannibal, MO: Granted Ministries Press, 2011), 133.

21. Geoff Thomas, 'The Preacher's Progress' in *A Marvelous Ministry: How the All-Round Ministry of Charles Haddon Spurgeon Speaks to Us Today*, (Ligonier, PA: Soli Deo Gloria Publications, 1993), 47.

When Lloyd-Jones was called to pastor the church at Sand-fields, they were expecting someone to come in with bright new ideas and save their church from a constant decline. They never anticipated what they had coming with Lloyd-Jones. The church at Sandfields had sought to answer their problem of decline through various activities such as football, musical events, and a dramatic society.

Some members approached Lloyd-Jones and suggested that they could be successful if they majored on their children's ministry. However, to their surprise, the new pastor wasn't interested in using such *things* to attract people. In fact, the secretary was very surprised at Lloyd-Jones' response to the question of his direction and the needs of the church. He was interested in the regular church services of 11am, 6pm, a Monday evening prayer service, a mid-week worship service on Wednesday, and a Saturday morning men's meeting. According to Lloyd-Jones, all of the other *things* could go. When the Committee asked what they were to do with the wooden stage for the dramatic society, Lloyd-Jones responded by saying, 'You can heat the church with it.'[22]

D. Martyn Lloyd-Jones did the hard thing at first by addressing the failed attempts of church growth and broken strategies of man. His decisions were not popular. In fact, when the Doctor announced that there would be no more stage dramas in the hall, a Mrs Robson said to herself, 'You'll learn young man, you'll learn!' However, as she would later tell her story, she said, 'It was I who learnt.'[23] Lloyd-Jones had an unshakable commitment to the Scriptures as the single weapon in the hands of the preacher that could bring about holy results.

---

22. David Martyn Lloyd-Jones, *The First Forty Years 1899–1939*, (Edinburgh: The Banner of Truth Trust, 2012), 135.

23. ibid., 210.

In our modern era, we likewise stand upon the shoulders of faithful men. One such man, with great influence among the movement known as New Calvinism is Mark Dever. In his excellent book titled, *Nine Marks of a Healthy Church*, Dever provides us with a good reminder regarding our need for the Bible. He writes:

> God's Holy Spirit creates His people by His Word. We can create a people by other means, and this is the great temptation of churches. We can create a people around a certain ethnicity. We can create a people around a fully-graded choir program. We can find people who will get excited about a building project or a denominational identity. We can create a people around a series of care groups, where each feels loved and cared for. We can create a people around a community service project. We can create a people around social opportunities for young mothers or Caribbean cruises for singles. We can create a people around men's groups. We can even create a people around the personality of a preacher. And God can surely use all of these things. But in the final analysis the people of God, the church of God, can only be created around the Word of God.[24]

When the apostle Paul was in Athens, he reasoned with the philosophers and skeptics of his day (Acts 17). He boldly proclaimed the resurrection of Jesus Christ to a group of urbane modernists who prided themselves in their intellectual acumen. Paul was not ashamed to align himself with the crucified and bloody Jesus. Paul was not intimidated to publicly embrace the resurrected Lord. The battle-tested servant of Christ called the self righteous and arrogant intellectual crowd to repentancee. Paul said, 'The times of ignorance God overlooked, but now he commands all people everywhere to repent, because he has fixed a day on which he

---

24. Mark Dever, *Nine Marks of a Healthy Church*, (Crossway, 2000), 36.

will judge the world in righteousness by a man whom he has appointed; and of this he has given assurance to all by raising him from the dead' (Acts 17:30-31 ESV). Some people believed Paul's message, however, the chapter ends by telling us that people mocked Paul as he passionately called them to repent.

We must never forget that the world will laugh at our gospel. It is time to stop appeasing the culture or seeking to win the affection of our society. The world will never think that Christianity is cool. However, we must remain steadfast, immovable, always abounding in the work of the Lord knowing that our labor is not in vain in Christ Jesus (1 Cor. 15:58).

When our culture laughs at our gospel, we must not apologize, dumb down, or so contextualize the gospel that the offense of the cross is veiled from the eyes of sinful men. We must do the work of discipleship, apologetics, evangelism, missions, and gospel preaching with the confidence that God's Word is our authority and as ambassadors of the King – we will not remain silent.

The battle cry of the Reformation was *sola Scriptura*. May it be said of us that we are people of the Book – unflinching on the inerrancy, authority, and sufficiency of God's Word. The battle over the Bible continues today, will you be found faithful?

The central character of John Bunyan's *The Pilgrim's Progress* is a man named Christian. Do you recall how he was pictured in the story? He was depicted as having the world behind him, heaven before him, and a Book in his hand. God has raised up many courageous champions of the faith from history and we can pray that God will continue to raise up men, women, boys, and girls within the New Calvinism movement who have the conviction of a Paul, the courage of a lion, and who will stand fearlessly in an age of compromise – with the world behind them, heaven before them, and a Book in their hands.

Sola Scriptura

2

Ecclesiology – The Church, Her Ministers, and *Sola Scriptura*

Paul Washer

MOST people are introduced to the Reformed faith through the doctrine commonly known as sovereign grace or Calvinism. This has often led to a great error in thinking that a person has embraced the Reformation simply because he has embraced this particular doctrine. Such a belief fails to recognize that the foundation stone of the Reformation is not a sovereign grace soteriology, but the doctrine of *sola Scriptura* (i.e. Scripture alone), and it is from this doctrine that the doctrine of sovereign grace was rediscovered. Thus, a person has not embraced the Reformed faith merely because he is Calvinistic in his soteriology, but because he has embraced the doctrine of *sola Scriptura* and is seeking to apply it to every aspect of his faith and practice.

We must admit that the Reformed faith has always included individuals who were not wholly likeminded. Luther and Calvin most certainly did not agree on all fronts, and yet they are considered fathers or patriarchs of the Reformation. After them we have the Puritans, such as Owen, Sibbes, Boston, Flavel, and a tinker named Bunyan, all of whom wrote and preached in a common stream but not without their differences. Finally, we move on in history to Edwards, Whitefield, Spurgeon, and Dr Martyn Lloyd-Jones – all great heirs of the Reformers in their own right, and possibly the last children of the Puritans – but even they would not be without a disagreement or two. What was the mortar of their unity and what was it about them that causes us to acknowledge their right of membership among the Reformed? I submit that, above all other doctrines and practices, it was their common commitment to *sola Scriptura* and its application to their lives and ministries. They sought to conform every aspect of their lives before God to the written Word of God. This brings us to a troubling and revealing question that we must ask about ourselves: 'Would the Reformers identify us as their heirs or even their children if they were to make a careful survey of our lives and ministries?' Would they be satisfied with the evidence that we are truly part of their lineage simply because we read their books, build monuments to them, attend conferences about them, and are 'Calvinistic' in our soteriology? Or would they scold us for having missed the main point altogether – that we are to diligently labor not only to study the Scripture but also to submit every aspect of our lives to its doctrine, wisdom, commands, and precepts?

One of the most outstanding characteristics of a reformation is that it does not assume that things are right merely because they have been practiced for a long, long time. Instead, everything – even the most long-standing and sacred cows of contemporary practice – is to be judged according to the sacred canon of God's Word, and if something does not measure up, it is either reformed or discontinued altogether.

It is for this reason that any true reformation requires not only great wisdom and tact, but also boldness, zeal, and tenacity. With a biblical diligence, guided by love and wisdom, we are to leave no stone unturned, but to examine every doctrine and practice under the lens of Scripture. Then we are not merely to write theological treatises to be examined and debated, but to make real changes in our own personal lives and in the Lord's church.

In this spirit of the Reformation, let us ask ourselves how thorough our personal reformation truly is. We boast of a Reformed soteriology, but how much of it has impacted our evangelism, our proclamation of the gospel, and our invitation to sinners to come to Christ? It matters little how many 'right books' we have in our libraries if our knowledge of the true gospel has not actually affected what and how we preach. Is our gospel preaching God-centered? Does it expose men to what the Scriptures truly say about man and his terrible predicament? Are the great doctrines of propitiation, redemption, regeneration, repentance, and faith set before the people with a clarity and simplicity borne out of due diligence in our studies and private prayer? Do we merely give lectures about the gospel or, with Richard Baxter, do we 'preach as never sure to preach again and as a dying man to dying men'?[1] Have we schooled our congregants in the great doctrines of the gospel so that even the least among them has no need to find recourse in the trite and often dangerous evangelistic methodologies of the day?

We boast of a Reformed theology, but how much of it has affected our pastoral labor? Again, would our counseling and private instruction have any resemblance to the guidelines set forth in Baxter's *Reformed Pastor* or his *Christian Directory*?

---

1. *Baxter's Poetical Fragments* (1st ed,; 1681, p. 40, lines 7-8).

Would Ichabod Spencer recognize us as like-minded brethren in the counseling of lost souls?[2] Have we followed Matthew Henry in his diligence to ensure the instruction of children so that 'the promise [that all shall know God from the least, even to the greatest] may be fulfilled and all pious endeavors for the propagating of Christian knowledge, crowned with success'?[3] Would Charles Bridges find our ministries to be positive or negative illustrations of his treatise on the *Christian Ministry with an Inquiry into the Causes of its Inefficiency?* Most importantly, have we, like the great Reformers and their heirs before us, gone to the one and only infallible guideline for ministry and labored to conform the goals, strategies, and daily activities of our ministries to its precepts? We must remember that reformers are not merely thinkers, treatise writers, or those involved in dialog; but they actually change things!

Let us go farther and look at our personal devotional life. We boast of having a Reformed or Puritan theology, but do we have their piety, their meditation on the Scriptures, and their life of prayer? Can anything of the diligence of John Calvin, Jonathan Edwards, or J. C. Ryle be seen in our study? Has Goodwin's instruction in prayer made us more useful in prayer?[4] Has the prayer life of David Brainerd[5] or Robert Murray M'Cheyne[6] done anything more than convict us of our lack of prayer? Has moral purity truly become a topic of

---

2. Ichabod Spencer (1798–1854) is the author of *A Pastor's Sketches: Conversations with Anxious Souls Concerning the Way of Salvation.*

3. Matthew Henry's *Plain Catechism for Children*, Introduction.

4. *Return of Prayers*, found in Thomas Goodwin's *Works*, vol. 3, p. 353-423.

5. *The Life and Diary of David Brainerd*, edited by Jonathan Edwards.

6. *The Memoir and Remains of The Reverend Robert Murray M'Cheyne* by Andrew Bonar.

intense concern to those of us who claim to love the Puritans? After all, they were not called 'puritans' for nothing! Like them, have we set out to discover in the Scriptures that which God hates in order that we might avoid it with all our might? Have we endeavored with the same intensity to become intimately acquainted with all that God loves and to embrace it until we become one with it?

What about our family life? Surely, we have learned from all our reading that this was a matter of great concern to the Reformers, Puritans, and early Evangelicals whom we admire. The Scriptures themselves tell us that if we do not manage our own household well we prove not to be mature Christians and we do not even qualify for the Christian ministry.[7] But how can we know how to manage our own households well without a sure word from the Scriptures? And how can we have that sure word unless, like the Reformers before us, we return to the Scriptures and reform our family structure, relationships, devotion, education, and discipline in light of them? Surely these things are worth the time it takes to consider them in light of God's Word! What does God really say about the role of the husband and wife? How are children to be raised? What are the biblical parameters within which we are allowed to walk freely?

Finally, we boast of a Reformed theology, but how much of it has affected the way we care for God's church? Although our stewardship of our wives and children is weighty, the stewardship of God's house is weightier still. How much time as ministers and elders have we given to wrestling over

---

7. 1 Timothy 3:4-5 – 'He *must be* one who manages his own household well, keeping his children under control with all dignity (but if a man does not know how to manage his own household, how will he take care of the church of God?' (NASB). See also Titus 1:6.

what God has commanded in His Word regarding His own Bride and the expressions of that Bride in the local assembly? Like the incorrigible renegades of the Old Testament period of the judges, have we done that which is right in our own eyes?[8] Both the Scriptures and history tell us that following our own wisdom is not a wise thing to do! What a terribly dangerous privilege it is to be an overseer of God's Bride and children. How foolish and reckless is the man who seeks to do so outside the parameters of God's Word. How rash is the man who has set his mind to dress God's Bride in any gown but the one that He gave to her!

Many questions have been raised in the last several lines, and each of them is worthy of its own treatise, but we have space to set upon only one of them. However, if we learn to properly apply the principle of *sola Scriptura* to this one great theme that we are about to address, surely the wisdom will bleed over into the rest of our lives and ministries. The theme of this chapter is 'Ecclesiology: The Church, Her Ministers, and *Sola Scriptura*.' In the next few pages, and in the light of the Scriptures, we will consider the importance of the local assembly, the ownership of the local assembly, the infallible guide of the local assembly, and the duty of the minister of the local assembly.

The Importance of the Local Assembly

In a truly Reformed tradition, we will begin by stating that before the foundation of the world was laid, God contrived a plan to get glory for Himself through a people that He would redeem. He elected them before the foundation of the world[9] to be redeemed through a Savior who was foreknown

---

8. Judges 17:6; 21:25.

9. Ephesians 1:4.

before the foundation of the world.[10] And He purposed from all eternity that this manifold wisdom, which for ages had been hidden in God,[11] would be brought to light through the church,[12] and that He would be glorified 'in the church and in Christ Jesus to all generations forever and ever' (NASB).[13] Charles Hodge writes:

> The works of God manifest His glory by being what they are. It is because the universe is so vast, the heavens so glorious, the earth so beautiful and teeming, that they reveal the boundless affluence of their Maker. If then, it is through the church that God designs specially to manifest to the highest order of intelligence, His infinite power, grace and wisdom, the church in her consummation must be the most glorious of His works.[14]

The Scriptures teach that the church is the pinnacle of God's works and the great revelation of His manifold wisdom; but is this great compliment directed only to some universal church or to the church triumphant in heaven, or is it given

---

10. 1 Peter 1:20.

11. Charles Hodge argues correctly that, 'The mystery or secret, is not the simple purpose to call the Gentiles into the church, but the mystery of redemption. This mystery, from the beginning of time, had been hid in God.' He sights as proof other Pauline texts which speak of the same mystery in an application that is far wider than the Gentiles (Rom. 16:25; 1 Cor. 2:7; Col. 1:26). He then writes, 'In all these places the mystery spoken of is God's purpose of redemption, formed in the counsels of eternity, impenetrably hidden from the view of men until revealed in His own time' (Charles Hodge, *A Commentary on the Epistle to the Ephesians* (Accordance electronic ed. New York: Robert Carter and Brothers, 1856), 169-170.

12. Ephesians 3:9-11.

13. Ephesians 3:21.

14. Charles Hodge, *A Commentary on the Epistle to the Ephesians* (Accordance electronic ed. New York: Robert Carter and Brothers, 1856), 174.

equally to the local assembly of believers here on earth? The entire course of Paul's ministry would indicate that the local assembly is more than included, for it was for the sake of real people gathered in real local assemblies in real places scattered throughout Asia Minor and Europe that Paul labored so strenuously during his time on earth. They were not large in number, they were 'not many wise according to the flesh, not many mighty, not many noble' (NASB),[15] but the apostle Paul saw them as the great means through which the glory of God was and is revealed to both men and angels. It is for this reason that we argue that to neglect the local assembly and its spiritual prosperity is to neglect God's greatest plan on earth to reveal His glory.

There is much for which to praise God about the resurgence of the Reformed faith throughout the world, especially among young people. However, there are also many troubling signs that not all is well in Zion. It seems that a significant number of the newly Reformed are often more enamored with doctrine, celebrity teachers, Bible conferences, and mission agencies than they are with the local church and her ministers. While at least some of the things just mentioned can be very helpful, they are *not* God's primary means of advancing the gospel, caring for His people, or revealing His glory to men or angels. God's plan is the local church. Why then is she so often neglected and passed over? Possibly for the same reason that the typical housewife cannot compete with the supermodel or actress on stage or screen. The housewife is real, with faults and defects exposed, but the actress is made up and decorated. The housewife is the stuff of everyday life, but the actress is seen only in the most attractive role and at the most spectacular moments. Similarly, the local

---

15. 1 Corinthians 1:26.

church is something that is real, exposed, and undecorated. A congregation of redeemed people caught in time between the already and the not yet; new creations that are not quite fully new; pilgrims on the road to Zion, but still marred in part by the soil of Babylon. The conference is different. It is filled with likeminded people even in the most intricate nuances of the faith, and they are all appearing on their very best behavior – no misunderstandings, bickering, or outbursts of immaturity. Three or four days of heaven on earth! Then there are the conference speakers. They have published more books than the local pastor has read, they are educated and eloquent, and their sermons are full of the most intricate theological wonders. They appear suddenly upon the platform, speak with the lips of a seraph, and then are whisked away like Elijah in a chariot of fire.[16] But the minister of the local church knows no such glory. He lives in anonymity to the larger Christian community and yet is under the constant scrutiny of his people day after day and year after year. He has three messages a week to prepare, private counseling sessions, visits to the hospital, and a constant battle with fatigue and doubt. He is a shepherd guarding a handful of sheep, a lonely sentinel on a night watch, a steward who gives God's servants their rations at the proper time.[17] Like his Master, he has no stately form or majesty that we should look upon him, nor appearance that we should be attracted to him.[18] For these reasons and many more unmentioned, it is not difficult to see why the young and the immature will be enamored with the conferences, YouTube speakers, and the great authors and musicians of our day. But the discerning eye will see the

---

16. 2 Kings 2:11.

17. Luke 12:42.

18. Isaiah 53:2.

wisdom and power of God in the local congregation and the men who faithfully serve there.

We should praise God for Bible conferences and the helpful preachers who are often used so mightily in them. We should also praise God for the Internet and the bountiful supply of good preaching that can be found there. However, these things should never compete with our devotion to the local church and the pastors who care for our souls. Jesus' admonition to the undiscerning crowd is applicable to us all: 'Do not judge according to appearance, but judge with righteous judgment' (NASB).[19] A great theologian was once asked, 'Who is the greatest preacher alive today?' He responded, 'Whoever he is, you don't know him.' Another old preacher once said, 'Some of the greatest sermons that have ever been preached were preached to only six people.' It is a truth well known among the mature that God often hides His best men and His best works from a greater audience. Why would God plant the most beautiful rose He has ever created in a forest through which no man or angel will ever walk? How can He receive glory from something that is so hidden? Answer: He receives glory because it is not hidden from Him, and He looks upon it with great delight!

It is interesting that with regard to our participation in meetings outside of the local church we are not given any certain command in the Scriptures. Yet with regard to our participation in the local church, the command of Scripture is clear and touches every saint of God. In Hebrews 10:24-25 we read:

> Let us consider how to stimulate one another to love and good deeds, not forsaking our own assembling together, as is the

---

19. John 7:24.

habit of some, but encouraging *one another;* and all the more as you see the day drawing near (NASB).

This text is proof positive that if we are not committed to a local congregation of believers we are not walking in the center of God's will. The key word here is 'committed.' The command is not fulfilled by mere attendance but by our active participation in the growth and sanctification of the body. We should never think that we are doing God's will simply because we attend a church with sound theology and expository preaching and are frequently involved in theological conversations with our peers. We are committed when we are actually ministering in the church under the direction of the elders and for the sake of the least of Christ's brethren,[20] even those who do not share our interest in high theological dialog, but are simply struggling to make it down the road to Zion. If we do not love the most broken, needy, and theologically inept brethren in the local church, then our love for the church and for Christ Himself is in question.

If you are young and 'Reformed,' I would plead with you to start your journey into truth and Christlikeness within the context of the local church and under the care of a pastor or pastors whose lives are worthy of imitation, who preach the truth, and who truly care for your soul. I would also plead with you to understand that your theology is only as good as your piety and your love for the local church, manifested in acts of self-denial and service to the least of Christ's brethren.

The Ownership of the Local Assembly

There is no minister in his theologically right-mind who would conscientiously deny that the Owner of the church is

---

20. Matthew 25:31-40.

God. And yet, it appears from the admonitions of Scripture that ministers still have a great need of being reminded of this truth. Paul gave the following warning to the overseers in Ephesus:

> Be on guard for yourselves and for all the flock, among which the Holy Spirit has made you overseers, to shepherd the church of God which He purchased with His own blood (NASB).[21]

Notice that Paul not only declares the church to be God's possession, but he also sets forth the means by which this possession was obtained – 'with His own blood.' As in 1 Peter 1:18-19, the reference to the atonement and, more specifically, the blood of the Son of God denotes more than mere ownership; it also communicates the great worth of the church to God.[22] Since His Bride was purchased at such a great cost, she must be of inestimable value to Him. Consequently, He must be very jealous for her and adverse to all who would cross boundaries and take liberties with her that they were never given. We should not think it unusual that the One who will not share His glory with another[23] is equally unwilling to share the greatest manifestation of His glory (i.e. the church) with another[24] not even with the ministers or stewards who have been placed in charge of her.

In Paul's first letter to his young disciple Timothy, he is even more explicit regarding the church as God's possession:

---

21. Acts 20:28.

22. 1 Peter 1:18-19 – 'Knowing that you were not redeemed with perishable things like silver or gold from your futile way of life inherited from your forefathers, but with precious blood, as of a lamb unblemished and spotless, *the blood* of Christ' (NASB).

23. Isaiah 42:8.

24. Ephesians 3:9-11.

> I am writing these things to you, hoping to come to you before long; but in case I am delayed, I write so that you will know how one ought to conduct himself in the household of God, which is the church of the living God, the pillar and support of the truth (NASB).[25]

Again, notice how adamant Paul is that Timothy understands both the truth and application of God's ownership of the church. In true Hebrew fashion, he uses repetition to drive home the point – it is the 'household of God,' 'the church of the living God, the pillar and support of the truth.' There is enough wisdom revealed in these three descriptions that if they were obeyed by the great majority of ministers in the evangelical community, it would heal much of what ails us in the church today. For this reason, it will benefit us to take a closer look.

The description of the church as the 'household of God' denotes not only ownership but also spousal, parental, and familial affection. God loves the church as His bride, children, and family. The great truth for God's ministers to take from this title is that the church is *God's* house, and consequently, it is to be run by *His* rules.

The description of the church as the 'church of the living God' draws a powerful contrast between the church and the pagan temples in the city of Ephesus, where countless false gods were enshrined.[26] This description also adds a great deal of Old Testament solemnity to our view of God's relationship to the church. The church belongs to 'the true God; He is the living God and the everlasting King. At His

---

25. 1 Timothy 3:14-15.

26. The phrase 'living God' is often used in Old Testament in contrast to the false gods of the nations (Jer. 10).

wrath the earth quakes, and the nations cannot endure His indignation' (ESV).[27] He is not to be taunted[28] or reproached,[29] as pagan enemies such as Goliath and Sennacherib quickly learned. Nor are we His people to do what is right in our eyes in matters that pertain to Him and His church, as Nadab and Abihu[30] and even good Uzzah[31] discovered at great cost. If God demonstrated such zeal and protective jealousy for a tabernacle and an ark sprinkled with the blood of bulls and goats,[32] how much more zeal and jealousy does He have for the church that was purchased with His own blood! Yes, this title 'church of the living God' should produce in any discerning minister a cautious lip and trembling hand.

A few years ago, a very well-known and accomplished business magnate renounced any relation to the Christian God because of the scriptural declaration that He is jealous. To illustrate the arrogance and irrationality of this magnate, imagine that an upstart employee walked into the central office and began to reorganize and reshape everything. Would this magnate be pleased? Would he or she not put a stop to the matter with great offense and indignation? Would he or she not be right in doing so? How *dare* this hireling, who had nothing to do with the birth of the company, who made no great investment or contribution, be so presumptuous, brazen, and shameless! The employee's actions would certainly be met with an immediate and fierce dismissal. In light of this simple illustration, should not the living and true God be jealous for

---

27. Jeremiah 10:10.

28. 1 Samuel 17:26, 36.

29. 2 Kings 19:4, 16; Isaiah 37:4, 17.

30. Leviticus 10:1-3.

31. 2 Samuel 6:6-11.

32. Hebrews 10:4.

that which He has made and sustains? Should He not be even more jealous for the church that He bought by the blood of His own Son and that He intricately designed to manifest His glory? How *dare* any of God's ministers – no matter how great, gifted, or accomplished – be so presumptuous, brazen, and shameless so as to think they have the right to redesign or reshape the church according to their own opinion or according to the whims of a fallen, self-saturated, and grossly superficial culture! Such a minister will certainly be met with an immediate and fierce dismissal before the throne of God! Perhaps the most foolish and arrogant sin of God's ministers is that of doing what is right in their own eyes. It is strictly forbidden for the individual Christian to live outside the direct commands of Scripture, and those who ignore this do so at their own peril. But how much greater is the crime when God's ministers, mere stewards, take it upon themselves to redesign and redirect God's Bride and children in ways in which they have no authority to do so?

Finally, the description 'pillar and support of the truth' reminds us that the church 'holds up and supports the truth before the world, and maintains the truth in opposition to all attacks upon it.'[33] In his commentary on this phrase, Calvin writes, 'She is called "the pillar of truth" because the office of administering doctrine, which God hath placed in her hands, is the only instrument of preserving the truth, that it may not perish from the remembrance of men.'[34] There is a reason why the church should be so reluctant to modernize, refashion, or revamp itself. It is because she is founded upon the immutable or unchanging truth of God, and it is her task to set this truth before the world as absolute truth that does

---

33. D. Edmond Hiebert, *Everyman's Bible Commentary*, 1 Timothy, p. 73.
34. *Calvin's Commentaries*, vol. 21, 1 Timothy, p. 90.

not bend to the whims and desires of ever-changing fallen men and their ever-changing cultures. Regarding the Papists of his day Calvin writes:

> They do not consider that the truth of God is maintained by the pure preaching of the gospel; and that the support of it does not depend on the faculties or understandings of men, but rests on what is far higher, that is, the simple word of God.[35]

Can this crime that Calvin lays upon the Papists not also be levied against many evangelical ministers and even some among the camp of the Reformed? We live in an age that is permeated with pragmatism and the cleverness of men. Many of the church-planting books that are sold in the Christian market have to do with clever strategies that are blatantly and unapologetically borrowed from the secular world. Others amass a multitude of proof texts and take them out of context to validate a strategy that is foreign to the truth and spirit of the Scriptures. Still others are founded upon the principles of some extremely clever leader, who by using them was able to produce a megachurch within only a few years. Furthermore, it is promised that the same principles, applied in the same way, will produce the same results. Still others have decided that if the world will not come closer to the church, then we ought to bring the church closer to the world. Worship is replaced with entertainment, the mystery of godliness is replaced with self-realization and self-fulfillment, and piety is denounced as puritanical. The church no longer stands in contrast to Bunyan's Vanity Fair, but in competition with it! Finally, the most dangerous invention – and the one that seems to have taken many reformed brethren by storm –

---

35. *Calvin's Commentaries*, vol. 21, 1 Timothy, p. 91.

has to do with presenting the church to the world not as the pillar and support of the truth, but as intellectual, cultural, and cool. In such cases, the scandal of the gospel is lost, freedom becomes licentiousness, and much time is wasted trying to convince the world that we are not as ignorant, unsophisticated, and unhip as it thinks we are. In the end, the world is not convinced, and we just look silly!

Dear brothers, the church is the Bride of Jesus Christ, and she is precious to Him. He has given us clear direction in the Scriptures regarding how she is to be guided and presented to the world. How dangerous to neglect His infallible instruction for our clever inventions. Imagine that a great king had a bride who was precious to him above all his kingdom, and before going on a long journey, he entrusted her care to his steward. What an honor, and yet, what a terrifying responsibility! At the journey's end, the king returns to find that that the steward had ignored his instructions and substituted his own clever schemes. While the king was away, the steward noticed that the people were straying farther and farther from their loyalty to him and his precepts. They were no longer endeared to the queen, for she seemed outdated, uninteresting, and all too prudish. Thus, the steward convinced her to take off her plain white gown and replace it with something that would be more attractive to the people of the day. He let down her hair and painted her face with the most exaggerated tones. He taught her to walk and talk and entertain in a way that would draw back even the basest crowd, and then he paraded her before them as a lure. What would be the reward for the steward's cleverness when the king returned? His rage would be beyond telling, and his vengeance beyond words!

I fear that this will be the fate of many pastors whom God has put in charge of the care of His Bride. Unlike faithful Hegai in his custody of Esther,[36] they have not labored to make her attractive to her Husband and King, but to the crowds. For the last several decades we have seen foolish little men neglect the clear instruction of how Christ's most precious Bride is to be dressed, handled, and presented before the world. As cultures have grown more and more wicked, men who should know better have sought to redress the Bride of Christ in such a way that she might be attractive to carnal men; thus, they attempt to lure them back to God with a bride that is more to their liking. It is not the atheist or the murderer or the prostitute who has the most to fear on that Final Day, but the pastors, who like unreasoning animals[37] with no fear of the Lord gave God's Bride a carnal makeover that she might be attractive to the unregenerate. In light of all of this, it would be helpful for us to heed the words of the great Reformer John Calvin regarding Paul's instruction to Timothy in 1 Timothy 3:15:

> By holding out to pastors the greatness of the office, he undoubtedly intended to remind them with what fidelity, and industry, and reverence they ought to discharge it. How dreadful is the vengeance that awaits them, if, through their fault, that truth which is the image of the Divine glory, the light of the world, and the salvation of men, shall be allowed to fall! This consideration ought undoubtedly to lead pastors to tremble continually, not to deprive them of all energy, but to excite them to greater vigilance.[38]

The Infallible Guide of the Local Assembly

Having settled the matter of ownership, we can now turn our attention to the matter of how Christ's church should be

---

36. Esther 2:8-9, 15.

37. Jude 10.

38. *Calvin's Commentaries*, vol. 21, 1 Timothy, p. 90.

guided. Notice again Paul's careful language to Timothy in 1 Timothy 3:15. In the few words of this unassuming text is found the entire doctrine of how Christ's ministers are to care for the church, but it is often overlooked to great peril:

> I write so that you will know how one ought to conduct himself in the household of God, which is the church of the living God, the pillar and support of the truth (NASB).[39]

The word 'conduct' comes from the Greek word *anastrépho*, which literally means, 'to overturn,' and by implication, 'to busy oneself' or 'behave oneself.' The absence of a pronoun in the original text makes it difficult to determine if Paul is referring to Timothy's conduct or that of believers in general, but as D. Edmond Hiebert points out, 'It makes little difference since Timothy's "behavior" or "manner of life" in carrying out the instructions would affect the behavior of the church.'[40] What an absolutely solemn and even terrifying thought for the discerning minister! The local church will in some measure take upon itself the doctrine, character, and piety of its ministers – for good or for evil. The minister who longs to have a greater and greater influence over the local church and the church at large through media, conferences, and other such things does not understand what he desires. In the words of Jesus, 'From everyone who has been given much, much will be required; and to whom they entrusted much, of him they will ask all the more' (NASB).[41] We should pray that our influence over the church would increase only to the degree that we increase in the fear of the Lord and

---

39. 1 Timothy 3:15.

40. D. Edmond Hiebert, *Everyman's Bible Commentary*, 1 Timothy, p. 72.

41. Luke 12:48.

in submission to what is written in His Word. Let there be no soiled r_g of flesh on our bodies and nothing of our own cleverness in our mouths; for as ministers we do have influence, and as ministers, we will be called to give an account before the throne of the living God with regard to how we have cared for His most precious possession!

How then can we know how to conduct ourselves in our care of God's household? It is only through what is written in His Word. It is only under the infallible guidance of *sola Scriptura*. Paul wrote to Timothy, 'I *write* so that you will *know* how one ought to conduct himself in the household of God.' Therefore, the more closely we submit ourselves to what is written, the clearer our conscience will be, and the more confidence we will possess. Consequently, the more we stray from the direct commands of Scripture and give ourselves to our own inventions, the more we open ourselves to Christ's reprimand.

In my years as a missionary in Peru, I often found myself in many dangerous places and predicaments in the jungle, in the inner city, and in the midst of a bloody civil war. I survived them all, but not by my cunning or expertise, for I was raised a farm boy in the flatlands of Illinois. I was not worldly wise, I knew nothing of the culture of the inner city, and I had no military or survival training so that I could have made it even one day on my own. So how did I survive? I survived by concluding that I knew nothing and by fully depending upon and submitting to my Peruvian brothers who were born in the jungle or were raised in the inner city or were experienced in survival. Many today have this erroneous idea that submission to authority brings limitations and even bondage, yet I have found the very opposite to be true. Submission to authority in Peru allowed me to go places, do things, and survive ordeals that would have otherwise been impossible.

So many Christian leaders today seem to believe that to throw away our trust in the arm of the flesh and to lean wholly upon what is written would severely limit the church's ability to impact the world, but nothing could be further from the truth! The more we cut ourselves off from the arm of the flesh, the more we will see the power of God, and the more this world will be impacted by truth. Furthermore, the more we abandon our own cleverness and trust in only what is written, the more likely we are not only to save others, but also to save ourselves. As Paul wrote Timothy, 'Pay close attention to yourself and to your teaching; persevere in these things, for as you do this you will ensure salvation both for yourself and for those who hear you' (NASB).[42] Regarding Paul's admonition to Timothy concerning how one ought to conduct himself in the household of God, Calvin writes:

> By this mode of expression he commends the weight and dignity of the office; because pastors may be regarded as stewards, to whom God has committed the charge of governing his house. If any person has the superintendence of a large house, he labors night and day with earnest solicitude, that nothing may go wrong through his neglect, or ignorance, or carelessness. If only for men this is done, how much more should it be done for God?[43]

With what I have written thus far, some may think that I have overstated God's scrutiny and future judgment of the minister and his stewardship or that I have promoted an unhealthy fear of judgment. Some may argue that I have been all too simplistic in thinking that everything we need for the direction for the church is found in what is written

---

42. 1 Timothy 4:16.

43. *Calvin's Commentaries*, vol. 21, 1 Timothy, p. 89.

in God's Word. Others may suppose that I have not given sufficient recognition to the common grace of God that enables ministers to apply what is written or think beyond it in order to adapt Christianity to a new age. However, let me remind you of two unalterable truths, whose interpretations are not open to debate. The first is that we will be judged, and for some ministers, this will result in the loss of everything except their souls. The second is that the only infallible standard by which we are to guide our conduct in the church is the written Word of God. The further we stray from it, and the more we take away from it or add to it, the less confidence we can have that we will pass through judgment unscathed. This is affirmed by Paul's words in 1 Corinthians 3:11-15:

> For no man can lay a foundation other than the one which is laid, which is Jesus Christ. Now if any man builds on the foundation with gold, silver, precious stones, wood, hay, straw, each man's work will become evident; for the day will show it because it is *to be* revealed with fire, and the fire itself will test the quality of each man's work. If any man's work which he has built on it remains, he will receive a reward. If any man's work is burned up, he will suffer loss; but he himself will be saved, yet so as through fire (NASB).

Dear brothers, read this text again and again until it resounds in your heart and mind like a trumpet. Read it prayerfully. Read it on your knees. Cry out for understanding and for the wisdom to apply what you understand in your care for God's Bride. It is more than possible that many who now read these lines will suffer great loss if they do not make radical changes before it is too late.

Since the Reformation, something of a battle has raged between those who hold to the Regulative Principle and those who hold to the Normative Principle. The former states that only those elements that are instituted by command or example or which can be rationally deduced from Scripture are permissible in worship. The latter teaches that whatever is not prohibited in Scripture is permitted in worship, as long as it promotes the peace and unity of the church. The purpose of mentioning these two principles is not to debate their virtues or vices but simply to state that, in light of 1 Timothy 3:14-15 and 1 Corinthians 3:11-15, it ought to be clear that the more we are inclined to the Regulative Principle, the more confident we can be that our care of God's church is pleasing to Him. By contrast, the further we stray toward the Normative Principle, the closer we come to opening a 'Pandora's Box' in the church, releasing all manner of dangers and bringing our ministries against the will of God. It is often remarked in rebuttal that even those in the Regulative camp have differences of opinions regarding what is truly allowed by Scripture. Although this is sometimes the case, it is still better to have men who are struggling, even debating, to discover the will of God revealed in the Scriptures than to have them guiding the church with little regard for the Scriptures. The most disturbing fact in this matter is not that there has been a debate between sincere ministers throughout much of the history of the church, but that many contemporary ministers have moved so far away from *sola scriptura* that they are totally unaware of the importance of the debate or they treat it as a matter of such little significance that they are indifferent to it.

The Minister's Duty to the Local Assembly

Why are God's ministers so prone to stray from His direct commands and follow their own inventions? Four major reasons come to mind. First, not all of those numbered among the ministers of Christ are truly converted. When we consider the boldness with which many of them neglect the Word of God and their obvious lack of the fear of the Lord, there can be only one explanation – they do not belong to Christ. Secondly, there is ignorance even among converted ministers about what the Scriptures teach regarding the minister's character, devotion, and duties within the church. Many were trained in Bible colleges and seminaries that gave only a nod to doctrine, church history, spiritual disciplines, and biblical ministry and were more concerned with pragmatic principles and strategies of church growth. Thirdly, even sincere and properly educated ministers can become so occupied with the minor things that they have little time before God in His Word and prayer. Finally, there is the matter of the flesh. God's way is hard on the flesh; and therefore, the flesh looks for a substitute at every turn. It is amazing how many hours a minister will give to strategic planning, organization, programs, and searching through books on leadership and the latest tactics on how to make the church relevant in the twenty-first century. But the study of Scripture is all but abandoned, and the prayer closet is vacant. God's way is often slow, and at times its benefits can only be seen through the eyes of faith. Programs are easier than painstaking preparations of the heart and the faithful proclamation of God's Word. Strategies are more tantalizing than hours and hours of both hidden and corporate prayer. A finely tuned and professional music ministry that can move the emotions is easier to achieve than a genuine visitation from God and an outpouring of the Holy Spirit.

What then are our duties as ministers of Christ's church? First, we must rid ourselves of the extracurricular activities of ministry – that is, of all that parades itself as Christian ministry but is not ordained or authorized by the Scriptures. There is more than enough for the minister to do within the will of

God without adding other duties that are outside His will. Secondly, we must give ourselves to what is commanded of us in the Scriptures, according to the priority that the Scriptures give each command. We must lash ourselves down to 'what is written.' Intuition is not enough to guide us through the labyrinth of distractions and dangers. Although by common grace we may be able to avoid the more extravagant errors, those that are subtler will catch us. We must remember that ministers are not often sidetracked by vile things, but by good things that are not the best. A wonderful example of this is found in Acts 6:2, 4. When confronted by the need of the widows in the church, the apostles declared:

> It is not desirable for us to neglect the word of God in order to serve tables.... But we will devote ourselves to prayer and to the ministry of the word (NASB).

The care of widows in the church cannot be neglected without arousing God's judgment. Nevertheless, it does not trump the greatest need in the church, which is for the church's leaders to be devoted to prayer and the ministry of the Word. Christ's ministers are not primarily charismatic figures, movers and shakers, or inventors of clever ideas. They are stewards who do only what their Master has commanded them and afterwards declare, 'We are unworthy slaves; we have done *only* that which we ought to have done' (NASB).[44] They are men of God, watching daily at His gates and waiting at His doorposts.[45] They live to know God and make Him known through the proclamation of God's Word in the street, the house, the pulpit, and the counselor's chair. Like

---

44. Luke 17:10.
45. Proverbs 8:34.

Ezra, they have set their heart to study the law of the Lord and to practice it, and to teach His statutes and ordinances in Israel.[46] Like Levi, they revere God and stand in awe of His name. True instruction is in their mouth, and unrighteousness is not found on their lips; they walk with Him in peace and uprightness and turn many back from iniquity. Their lips preserve knowledge, and men seek instruction from their mouth; for they are indeed messengers of the Lord of hosts.[47] They are followers or imitators of God in 'speech, conduct, love, faith and purity, showing themselves to be examples of those who believe' (NASB).[48] They are leaders who seek to guide the church into the very center of God's will, using the only means that God has given them to do so – *what is written!* When these things have become our 'stock-in-trade,' then we will truly be sons of the Reformation and heirs of the legacy of *sola Scriptura!*

---

46. Ezra 7:10.

47. Malachi 2:4-7.

48. 1 Timothy 4:12.

3

Holiness is Relevant

Steven J. Lawson

✣

IN recent decades, there has emerged a movement known as 'New Calvinism,' or as some have called it, 'Young, Restless, and Reformed.' This is a movement that has captured the hearts of countless Christians, young and old alike, drawing them back to the cardinal truths of biblical Christianity and, more specifically, to historic Calvinism. The core doctrines of sovereign grace that were once the theological high ground for the sixteenth century Reformation have once again been scaled and become the lofty heights upon which this new resurgence stands.

When we survey this movement, there is much to be praised. There has been a return to the five *solas* of our Protestant forefathers. These bold assertions, once affirmed by the German Reformer Martin Luther (1483–1546), the Genevan Reformer John Calvin (1509–1564), and many others, include *sola Scriptura*, *sola gratia*, *sola fide*, *solus Christus*, and *soli Deo gloria*. The Reformers taught that every doctrinal belief must be built upon Scripture alone, which asserts that salvation is by grace alone, through faith alone, in Christ alone. When these first four *solas* are firmly fixed, they lead inevitably to the glory of God alone. These foundational truths once again have been fully recovered by the New Calvinism and are now being fervently proclaimed.

In addition, this present day movement has affirmed the five doctrines of grace – total depravity, unconditional election, definite atonement, irresistible grace, and the perseverance of the saints. These biblical truths that once prevailed in the Protestant Reformation have been re-enlisted and sent into frontline action by the Young, Restless, and Reformed. The return to the exclusive authority of Scripture has led the way to the inevitable commitment to these historic Calvinistic doctrines.

Legions of foot soldiers – young preachers, foreign missionaries, church planters, seminary professors, Bible teachers, and lay people – have become the standard bearers of these Reformed truths. Their fidelity to the truth of God's Word, their commitment to the gospel of Jesus Christ, and their emblazoned desire for the glory of God is transforming this current generation of evangelicals around the globe. With the advent of modern technology to spread and proliferate this Reformed teaching, these are unprecedented days in the history of the church.

However, as we survey this new resurgence, we must ask ourselves, has the movement gone as far as it needs to go? Are the priorities of this movement where they need to be? Have all of the biblical doctrines been properly emphasized? The answers we give to these questions are critical because they will shape the long term trajectory of this influential evangelical movement. I do not write as an outside observer and critic of this movement. When Collin Hansen's book, *Young, Restless, and Reformed* first appeared in 2008, I am featured in his presentation of this theological resurgence. I write as one who has been identified with this movement and who has paid an enormous price, personally, to preach these Calvinistic doctrines. In short, I have skin in the game.

In the midst of this rising tide of truth, I see one specific truth that needs our careful attention. I refer to the doctrine of sanctification, or the pursuit of personal holiness. While the more highly emphasized doctrines of unconditional election, absolute predestination, and justification by faith alone have been recovered, there exist some deficiencies about how to live the Christian life. The Scripture, however, speaks with no such uncertainty. In fact, there is much more teaching in Scripture regarding how one is to live the Christian life than how one is to become a Christian.

How important is rightly addressing this subject of sanctification? The answer is, this doctrine is critically important. God is, first and foremost, more concerned with what He is doing *in* us than with what He is doing *through* us. He is fundamentally concerned with our godliness before He is with our giftedness. He is of first importance, more interested in our spirituality than in our productivity. This is to say, God is principally focused upon the depth of our maturity before the breadth of our ministry. Herein lies the importance of this subject.

One Holy Passion for God

That said, our innermost being must be driven by the desire to know God and follow Christ by the power of the Spirit. Every Christian must cultivate his own spiritual life before God in order to bring Him glory. This pursuit of holiness is precisely what the apostle Paul prioritized with Timothy, his young son in the faith, when he wrote, 'discipline yourself for the purpose of godliness' (1 Tim. 4:7 NASB). It is incumbent upon every Christian to discipline himself for godliness. We must fight to keep our minds pure by setting them on things above (Col. 3:2). We must resist every flaming arrow of the evil one in order to keep our hearts clean (Eph. 6:16). We must buffet our bodies (1 Cor. 9:27) if we are to keep our souls unstained by fleshly lusts (1 Pet. 2:11). We must be, as the young Scottish minister Robert Murray M'Cheyne (1813–1843) said, 'a pure instrument in the hand of God.'[1] This is to say, we must be a battle axe that is kept sharp and fit for our Master's use.

The Priority of Personal Holiness

As the apostle Peter writes his first letter to the scattered believers, he begins by calling them to pursue personal holiness in their daily lives. After the opening salutation and benediction, he immediately addresses the matter of their own godliness. He does so because this is of primary importance to this subject. Peter exhorts them:

> Therefore, prepare your minds for action, keep sober in spirit, fix your hope completely on the grace to be brought to you at the revelation of Jesus Christ. As obedient children, do not be conformed to the former lusts which were yours in your ignorance, but like the Holy One who called you, be holy yourselves also in all your behavior; because it is written, 'YOU SHALL BE HOLY, FOR I AM HOLY' (1 Pet. 1:13-16 NASB).

What the apostle writes to these persecuted believers underscores the priority of our own personal holiness. It is critical that we see the close and inseparable connection between election (1 Pet. 1:1-2), regeneration (1 Pet. 1:3), and sanctification

---

1. Robert Murray M'Cheyne, as quoted in Charles Spurgeon, *Lectures to My Students* (Carlisle, PA: Banner of Truth, 1875-94/2008), 2.

(1 Pet. 1:2, 13-16). God chose us and caused us to be born again in order to transform us into the image of Jesus Christ. It is crucial that we understand how this eternal purpose affects all that we are and do.

Within New Calvinism, there are, I perceive, many who are leery of this idea of holiness. Perhaps it sounds too puritanical for our modern tastes. Some quickly begin labeling any teaching on holiness as legalistic. Legalism is separating the law of God from the grace of God. When we isolate divine grace from divine law, we fail to see the infinite love of God that stands behind the commands He issues. When this unbiblical divorce takes place, we view His commands as burdensome, too heavy to bear. In many instances, the cancer of legalism spreads yet further and adds additional man-made regulations to Christian living that go beyond the written word of God. Consequently, there are well-meaning believers in this New Calvinism who have overreacted and swung the pendulum to the other extreme. They emphasize the liberty of the Christian life apart from obedience to the Scripture. In some cases, this had led to an abuse of Christian liberties.

As we begin exploring the subject of personal holiness, I want us to review a key passage in the opening section of Peter's first epistle. I want us to investigate 1 Peter 1:13-16 and consider what it requires from us.

A Strict Mind

First, the apostle Peter addresses the importance of the Christian mind. He says, 'prepare your minds for action' (NASB) (13). Literally, 'prepare' (*anazonnumi*) means 'to gird up.' It refers to gathering up one's long flowing robe in order to be unimpeded in movement before taking action. If someone wanted to move quickly, he would pull up the corners of his garment so that there would be nothing upon which he would trip his feet. He would tuck all the loose ends into the leather belt. Metaphorically, this pictured the call to each individual Christian to be prepared for action in his daily life. Peter is saying: 'Pull in all your loose thinking. Discipline your thoughts. Do not be tripped up by wrong beliefs. Do not allow any loose thinking to not be tied down with sound doctrine. All your thinking must be tucked in and tied down to the truth.'

This verb 'prepare' is in the imperative mood, meaning it is an authoritative command. All believers must obey this. Further, it is in the present tense, indicating we must be always keeping our mind tightly attached to truth. Moreover, it is in the third person plural, showing that this is the responsibility of all believers. In so doing, keeping this commandment is our duty and delight. Though regeneration is monergistic, involving only one Agent, who is God Himself, sanctification is synergistic involving two agents – God and man. This fact underscores our personal responsibility to follow this apostolic charge.

The apostle Paul uses this same imagery of preparing the mind when he addresses the spiritual warfare in which believers find themselves. He begins by making the same emphasis: 'stand firm therefore, having girded your loins with truth' (Eph. 6:14 NASB). In this analogy, the first thing a Roman soldier did before heading into battle was to enfold his loose flowing robe into his belt so that as he entered into battle he would not trip on it. When he girded up his robe, it indicated he was ready to enter into combat. A failure to do so meant he was easily defeated. To gird one's mind with truth is to know and understand the essential truths of the Word of God. There must be no loose thinking that is unattached to the Scriptures.

The battle for personal holiness begins with the battle for the Christian mind. Every aspect of living a holy life begins with sound thinking. Solomon writes, 'For as (the man) thinks within himself, so he is' (Prov. 23:7 NASB). In other words, what a person thinks is the fountain from which his entire life flows. The Bible places the first priority in godly living with a renewed mind. Sanctification initially requires being 'transformed by the renewing of your mind' (Rom. 12:2 NASB). We are charged, 'be renewed in the spirit of your mind' (Eph. 4:23 NASB). All growth in grace begins with having a mind that is saturated with the truth.

Saturated with the Scripture

Within the New Calvinism, there is a restored emphasis upon the singular authority and full sufficiency of the Word of God. That is clearly apparent and much to be applauded. There is a pervasive love of Scripture within this new generation of Reformed believers that desires to see God magnified in all things. However, it is common with some to be overly focused upon the passages that deal with joy, happiness, glory, and Christian liberty at the expense of those that speak about law, wrath, spiritual discipline, and divine chastisement. With others, there tends to be an approach to Scripture that neglects the hard sayings of Christ. Instead, if personal holiness is to be realized to its fullest extent, we must allow the whole counsel of God to be absorbed into our thinking.

To this very point, Martin Luther sought to be an ardent student of the entire Bible. In his own personal study, he repeatedly read through the Scriptures from cover to cover. No portion must be omitted. No truth unaddressed. Luther wrote, 'For a number of years I have now annually read through the Bible twice. If the Bible was a large, mighty tree and all its words were little branches, I have tapped at all the branches, eager to know what was there and what it had to offer.'[2] Such a comprehensive grasp of the Word should mark every growing believer. The entire message of Scripture must flood our mind if the fullness of its truths are to direct us into godliness.

Charles H. Spurgeon (1834–1892), expressed the same desire: 'It is blessed to eat into the very soul of the Bible until, at last, you come to talk in Scriptural language, and your very style is fashioned upon Scripture models, and what is better still, your spirit is flavoured with the words of the Lord.'[3] This is to say, every Christian must be saturated with the whole purpose of God in the whole of their being.

The English preacher, D. Martyn Lloyd-Jones (1899–1981) insists that there must be the regular, devotional reading of the Scripture from cover to cover:

> Read your Bibles systematically… I cannot emphasize too strongly the vital importance of reading the whole Bible…. Then, having done that, you can decide to work your way through one particular book, with commentaries or any aids that you may choose to employ…. read it because it is the food that God has provided for your soul, because it is the Word of God, because it is the means whereby you can get to know God. Read it because it is the bread of life, the manna provided for your soul's nourishment and well-being.[4]

This is where Christian holiness begins. It starts with our minds being prepared for action in personal godliness. We

---

2. *Luther's Works*, 54:165.

3. 'Mr Spurgeon as a Literary Man,' in *The Autobiography of Charles H. Spurgeon, Compiled from His Letters, Diaries, and Records by His Wife and Private Secretary*, vol. 4, 1878-1892 (Curtis & Jennings, 1900), p. 268.

4. Martyn Lloyd-Jones, *Preaching and Preachers* (London: Hodder & Stoughton, 1998), pp. 171-172.

must keep our minds free from the contaminations of this polluted world.

We must gird up the loins of our minds with the full counsel of God. There can be no loose thinking that is disconnected from the whole truth of Scripture. Neither can there be any doctrines neglected. Nor must there be worldly beliefs allowed to infiltrate our minds. We must master the whole truth of Scripture, and its whole truth, must master us.

A Sober Spirit

Second, the pursuit of personal holiness requires a sober spirit. Peter continues, 'keep sober in spirit' (NASB) (13). The word sober (*nepho*) literally means 'to be free from the influence of wine, to not become intoxicated.' Figuratively, the idea is not to come under the seductive sway of the world, the flesh, and the devil. To this point, we must not allow any sinful influence to dull our spiritual senses. We must never become mentally inebriated or emotionally unstable and lose control of our thinking. All who follow Christ must remain level headed in spirit. We must be temperate and discreet in our judgment. We must not allow anything to cause us to lose our spiritual balance as we walk in a manner worthy of our calling.

In other words, Peter is saying, 'Do not lose the sharp clarity of your thinking. Do not allow the seductions and allurements of the world to cause you to become spiritually inebriated and lose your moral equilibrium. Do not let the allurements of this world cause you to blur the lines between right and wrong.' This is to say, stay sober minded in your Christian living. Be serious about being holy. Be reverent toward God and filled with awe.

However, within some quarters, there appears to be a noticeable loss of sobriety. Being relaxed in worship appears to be a greater virtue than being reverent. Many in this movement believe we must maintain a worldly appearance in order to attract the world to the gospel. With this often comes a lighthearted approach to God. There is an intentional attempt to be laid back in the presence of God. Being glib in preaching is valued over having gravitas. I believe it can be shown that this casual thinking about God has led to the new casual worship of God. Moreover, the pulpit is more a dialogue than a declaration. A heavy dose of being sober in spirit is much needed medicine today.

This new tone toward God overemphasizes Christian liberty and underemphasizes the fear of God. Many assert that even the Ten Commandments are no longer in effect today. Some conclude that these divine laws, written by the finger of God, on tablets of stone, with letters of fire, have no bearing upon the New Testament Christian. This approach leaves believers with only the singular motivation of grace in Christian living. The fear of God is relegated to Old Testament times. Personal holiness, they claim, is not realized by a set of rules, commands, or a list of do's or don'ts. The grace of God supposedly has set us free from any codified restraints.

This unbalanced view of Christian freedom has led some within this movement to move dangerously close to antinomianism. This brand of lawless Christianity causes some to assume that the imperatives of Scripture are mere optional suggestions. This abuse of Christian liberty removes the protective boundaries that God in His goodness has established in His commandments. When the biblical imperatives are abandoned, the narrow path has no guardrails. The result is the countless fatal casualties of those who drive into a ditch or over a cliff.

Being sober in spirit in Christian living is critical to personal holiness. I sometimes hear a well-meaning Christian leader say, 'Do not take yourself too seriously.' That is bad counsel. This text teaches the very opposite. If we are to be holy as God is holy, we *must* take ourselves seriously. This mindset requires a sober spirit. Scripture calls us to be serious-minded as we walk before the Lord. Paul admonishes, 'let us cleanse ourselves from all defilement of flesh and spirit, perfecting holiness in the fear of God' (2 Cor. 7:1 NASB). Quite simply: no fear of God – no growth in holiness. Granted, the love of Christ should control us (2 Cor. 5:14), but the fear of God must also govern our soul. We must be 'knowing the fear of the Lord' (2 Cor. 5:11 NASB). Our awe of God must be a driving force in living a life of holiness.

A Steadfast Hope

Third, Peter adds that our growth in personal holiness requires a steadfast hope upon the future return of Christ. The apostle states, 'fix your hope completely on the grace to be brought to you at the revelation of Jesus Christ' (NASB) (13). The verb fix (*elpizo*) means to have a settled confidence about a future reality. The idea of hope is used today to mean wishful thinking about the future. For example, we say 'I hope it doesn't rain today.' However, in the Bible, the word hope means a fixed certainty about something in the future. It is being forward-looking toward an upcoming event with unwavering confidence. Biblical hope remains firm 'to the end' (*teleios*). Amid the surrounding moral pollution, Peter is saying, 'fix your hope' upon the return of Christ. This future reality elevates us to live on a higher, holier plane.

The apostle Peter issues this charge with an imperative verb. This indicates that this command comes with binding force upon us. Like a military officer who gives orders to his foot soldiers, so the apostle charges us to live accordingly. This authoritative charge commands us to fix our hope on the return of Christ. This is a suggestion, but an eternal perspective that is mandatory. This hope is to be fixed 'completely,' upon His return. That is, we must be looking entirely for His coming. There should be no distractions in our longing for His future appearing. Peter says, we must remain riveted upon this 'blessed hope' (Titus 2:13).

This future hope requires us to be fixed 'on the grace to be brought to you at the revelation of Jesus Christ.' This fast approaching 'grace' includes all that will be involved in the final state of our salvation, namely, glorification. This will be the final consummation and full realization of the saving purposes of God in our lives. When Peter writes that this transforming grace will 'be brought to you,' he is conveying that it will come to each believer in an intensely personal manner. Christ will come directly to each believer in a face-to-face encounter. It will be as if each Christian is the only individual for whom He is coming. This final consummation will occur at 'the revelation of Jesus Christ.' The word revelation (*apokalupsis*) means a disclosure or manifestation of what is hidden. It can also mean a laying bare or making naked. It represented the unveiling of what was previously unseen in order that it may be directly viewed. Presently, Jesus is invisible to us (1 Pet. 1:8). But at His return, He will be made visible, and we will look upon Him with glorified eyes.

At the appearing of Christ, we will be made like Him (1 John 3:2). There will require the complete eradication of our sinful body of flesh. All our sensual lusts and illegitimate desires will be permanently removed. No longer will we be plagued by selfish ambitions or sinful thoughts. The life long conflict with our flesh will be over. We will have a glorified spirit in a glorified body (Phil. 3:20-21). We will see Jesus Christ not as He once was, in His lowly state of humiliation. We will see Him as He presently is, in His exalted state of glorification. We will be perfected in holiness and enter into fullness of joy forever. All this and more is included in this final grace to be brought to us.

We must have this confident expectation riveted upon the imminent return of Christ. Too often, our attention is diverted to the pressing concerns and lures of this world. None of us is immune from becoming weighed down with the many demands in life that redirect our focus away from Him. These distractions can have a crippling effect upon our growth in godliness. We must remain focused upon the soon return of Christ.

With many today, the return of Christ can be a neglected subject. Why is this? Perhaps it is the differing eschatological positions that cause many to avoid this truth altogether. Perhaps it is because John Calvin never wrote a commentary on the book of Revelation. Perhaps it is because it is a complex subject. In this vacuum, there can be an overemphasis of looking backward to the sixteenth century Reformation. As a result, there can be a failure to be looking forward to the return of Christ. As glorious as the Protestant movement was, the return of Christ will be far greater. The different views of eschatology must never be allowed to prevent us from eagerly anticipating the return of the Lord. Whenever this lack of concentration occurs, our personal holiness suffers. If we are to be holy, we must be looking forward to the return of the Lord Jesus. 'And everyone who has this hope fixed on Him purifies himself, just as He is pure' (1 John 3:3 NASB).

Furthermore, some are little more than echo chambers for the tired mantra, 'All you need for sanctification is to look back and believe in your justification.' The implication is that this is the sum and substance of sanctification. But this is too simplistic. Sanctification is far more than merely looking back at your justification. Justification is only the foundation for our sanctification. A lifetime of construction work must build upon it. The pursuit of holiness requires looking ahead to our glorification as well. That is what the apostle Peter teaches in this verse. This forward look, longing for the coming of Christ must also be our gaze if we are to experience the fullness of sanctifying power.

A Submissive Will

Fourth, the apostle Peter stresses the necessity of our submissive will to God. He writes, 'As obedient children, do not be conformed to the former lusts which were yours in your ignorance' (NASB) (14). This verse addresses the readers as 'obedient children,' which could be rendered 'children of obedience.' The assumption is, if you are a child of God, your life will be marked by obedience. In other words, the distinguishing feature of a true child of God is a submissive will of obedience. 'Obedient' (*hupakoe*) means, 'to listen under.' The idea is to listen as one under authority. Today, we would say to listen up. Spiritually speaking, this means to give an attentive ear to what God says in His Word in order to obey Him. This requires maintaining a humble posture of submission under the authority of Scripture with a readiness to keep its commandments. Obedience from the heart is that which distinguishes a genuine Christian from a mere professing one.

This stress upon obedience, however, is often viewed today as legalism. Any emphasis on keeping the word can be denigrated as Phariseeism. They say, God desires a relationship, not a performance. While that is certainly true, the fruit of such a relationship will always be obedience. According to Scripture, obedience is one of the necessary evidences of any true believer. With stunning clarity, Jesus said, 'Not everyone who says to Me, "Lord, Lord," will enter the kingdom of heaven, but he who does the will of My Father who is in heaven will enter' (Matt. 7:21 NASB). If there is no obedience, there is no salvation. It is not the one who merely confesses Christ who is in the kingdom. Rather, it is the one who actively *does* the will of God. For the believer, such obedience is not a drudgery, but a delight (1 John 5:3).

In the larger theological spectrum, saving faith is inseparably connected to obedience. The apostle John writes, 'He who *believes* in the Son has eternal life; but he who does not *obey* the Son will not see life, but the wrath of God abides on him' (John 3:36 NASB, emphasis mine). Here we see that the polar opposite of saving faith is disobedience. We may rightly conclude that wherever there is faith in Jesus Christ, there is a new lifestyle of obedience to Him. Elsewhere, we read, 'faith, if it has no works, is dead, being by itself' (James 2:17 NASB). Calvin said, 'Faith alone saves. But faith that is alone does not save.'[5] Jesus 'became to all those who obey Him the source of eternal salvation.' An ongoing lifestyle of obedience is assumed. That is not legalism, but biblical Christianity.

Peter adds that we must 'not be conformed to the former lusts, which were yours in your ignorance' (NASB) (14). This points back to our pre-conversion life when we once lived in a state of continual sin. These 'former lusts' look back to the sinful desires, evil thoughts, and sensual appetites that previously dominated our lives. At that time, we lived in 'ignorance' without the knowledge of the holiness of God. But now, as Christians, we must not allow ourselves to be squeezed back into the mold of our former lusts. Our new life of obedience marks a dramatically changed course of life. We now must stay the course of holiness on which we presently find ourselves.

Each step forward in pursuing godliness requires a step of obedience to God. Disobedience to the Word is always a step

---

5. John Calvin, *Acts of the Council of Trent: with the Antidote*, 6th Session, can. 11.

backwards. This is sometimes called backsliding. A failure to keep the Word of God affects a spiritual advancement. Any marginalizing of personal obedience produces a stagnation, if not a reversal, in personal godliness. Whenever we are convicted of our own disobedience, we must immediately confess our sin with full repentance. The path on which we move forward in Christ-likeness is paved by obedience.

A Young Calvinist Who Pursued Holiness

The young, zealous pastor in Dundee, Scotland, Robert Murray M'Cheyne, flamed out for God at the young age of twenty-nine. He gave himself to the work of God as few men have given themselves to sacred endeavors. This young Calvinist said before he died, 'The greatest need of my people is my personal holiness.'[6] M'Cheyne understood that the effectiveness of his pastoral labors and pulpit ministry depended in large measure upon his personal godliness. M'Cheyne saw himself as a chosen instrument in the hand of a holy God, a minister who must be a pure instrument if he was to be effectively used.

M'Cheyne wrote to another pastor in his day, 'How diligently the cavalry officer keeps his saber clean and sharp. Every stain he rubs off with the greatest care. Remember, you are God's sword, His instrument. In great measure, according to the purity and perfection of the instrument will be its success.'[7] He then added, 'It is not great talents God blesses so much as great likeness to Jesus. A holy minister is an awful weapon in the hand of God.'[8] M'Cheyne rightly

---

6. Quoted by James Montgomery Boice, *Renewing Your Mind in a Mindless World: Learning to Think and Act Biblically* (Grand Rapids: Kregel Publications, 1993), 44.

7. Robert Murray M'Cheyne, as quoted in Charles Spurgeon, *Lectures to My Students* (Carlisle, PA: Banner of Truth, 1875-94/2008), 2.

8. ibid.

saw that the power of his ministry depended upon the purity of his life. M'Cheyne prayed, 'Lord, make me as holy as a pardoned sinner can be.'[9] Further, M'Cheyne concluded, 'Your whole usefulness depends on this.'[10]

The driving heartbeat of M'Cheyne for holiness must be the strong pulse within us. His passion for holiness must be our all-consuming passion. Down through the centuries, those who have been the most influential Christians have understood that their spiritual power has been largely dependent upon the purity of their lives. Nothing has changed in this present hour. God will only fill a holy vessel that has emptied itself of self.

This emphasis upon obedience is one that needs to be recovered in this new day. It is one thing to espouse the doctrines of grace, the five *solas*, and all the theological grandeur that accompanies Reformed theology. It is something else to put it into daily practice in a life of obedience. The truths in our head must be translated into the action of our hands and feet. Let me ask you: how important is obedience to you? Have the doctrines you profess to believe translated your life? Have they radically transformed the way you live your daily life? If not, what mind-course correction needs to take place in your life?

A Separated Life

Finally, Peter concludes this opening section by making an explicit call to a separated living. He writes, 'but like the Holy One who called you, be holy yourselves also in all your behavior' (NASB) (15). In this urgent plea, the apostle appeals to all believers to live in conformity to the holiness of God.

---

9. Andrew A. Bonar, *Memoir and Remains of Robert Murray M'Cheyne* (Banner of Truth Trust, 2009), 159.

10. ibid., 406.

Divine holiness is the primary attribute that describes the nature of God. Holiness is the only attribute singled out in Scripture that is repeated three times in describing God. The seraphim around the throne of God are crying out day and night, 'Holy, Holy, Holy, is the Lord of hosts' (Isa. 6:3 NASB). The same three-fold affirmation is also found in the New Testament (Rev. 4:8). By this thrice declaration, the holiness of God is elevated to the superlative level. Those in the immediate presence of God are declaring that God is holy, holier, holiest. That is, God is not merely holy. Neither is He simply holier than others. Instead, God is the holiest being in the universe. None is holy like God.

What does the holiness of God mean? The primary meaning of the holiness of God means that He is separate or set apart from all the works of His hands. It conveys the idea that God is high and lifted up above His creation. He is exalted and transcendent above all the universe. An enormous chasm separates God from this world. He is regal and majestic, clothed in splendor. The secondary meaning of the holiness of God is that He is set apart from all the defilements of sin. He is morally perfect in His being without the taint of any sin. He is entirely and utterly blameless in all His ways. In other words, everything about God is perfect. His being is perfect, His will is perfect, His judgments are perfect.

Consequently, this holy One has 'called' us to be holy as He is holy. That is an immensely high standard to which we are called. This divine call refers to the effectual summons of God issued to all His elect. It is a divine subpoena that apprehends those who are chosen for salvation and brings them to God. It is so powerful that it irresistibly overcomes all resistance in the day of God's power. This soul-arresting call draws us into a saving relationship with Him. This holy God who calls us also commands us. He demands our holiness. We are called by God in order to be conformed into the image of Christ. To be sure, we are saved to be sanctified.

So extensive is this apostolic command that Peter requires holiness 'in all your behavior' (15). No area of Christian living lies outside this. No aspect of our conduct is omitted from this. Our every action must be separated from sin and set apart unto righteousness. Charles Spurgeon said, 'There should be as much difference between the worldling and the Christian as between hell and heaven.'[11] That is, we are called out of the world to go back into the world, but we must not become of the world. We are not to live in isolation from the world. But we are to be insulated from the world.

Peter explains that holiness is not a new way to live. He writes, 'because it is written, "YOU SHALL BE HOLY, FOR I AM HOLY"' (16). In order to establish their pursuit of holiness, the apostle quotes Leviticus 11:44, 19:2, and 20:7 in order to show that this is rooted and grounded in the ancient text of the Old Testament. It is the commandment that God gave to Moses at Mount Sinai. In reality, it is what God said to Adam and Eve in the Garden. When God said they must not eat of the tree of the knowledge of good and evil, He was making a moral distinction between good and evil. God was setting before the first couple what is holy and what is unholy. God still makes His moral demands for separated living. Peter stresses this timeless command to live in separation from sin unto God.

To the contrary, many today are trying to become like the world in order to reach the world. Their desire appears to be to flirt with the world and court its approval. Some are

---

11. Charles Haddon Spurgeon, *Spurgeon's Sermons*, vol. 08 (Woodstock, Ontario: Devoted Publishing, 1863), 356.

adopting the edgy lifestyles of the pagan world. Some even mimic their salty language and crude jesting in the pulpit. They try to be more like a 'shock jock' than a holy man. Profanity is in, and purity is out. This crassness exists in spite of the fact that God says there must be no 'filthiness and silly talk, or coarse jesting' named among us (Eph. 5:4 NASB). Some leaders in the movement are involved in inappropriate relationships, marital separation, and unbiblical divorces as though this has no affect upon their qualification for ministry. But be assured, nothing could be further from the truth. The Word of God speaks without stuttering in the standard of holiness it requires. We must pursue purity of life with all of the strength God provides.

A Resolved Young Calvinist

One noted Christian minister who aggressively pursued personal holiness was the renowned Colonial Puritan of the eighteenth century, the venerable Jonathan Edwards (1703–1758). Edwards has become an iconic figure to many within the Young, Restless, and Reformed movement, and rightly so. This noted minister was a godly man worthy of our imitating. Many may not know about his ardent desire to live a life of godliness. At the young ages of eighteen and nineteen, Edwards wrote seventy resolutions that would serve as a moral compass for his spiritual life. He would read these statements of purpose as a way of staying on track in his pursuit of Christ-likeness. He resolved that he would live every day as though it were the last day of his life. In this effort, he was determined to discipline himself in the use of his time, tongue, and talents.

On January 14, 1723, young Jonathan Edwards, age nineteen, wrote Resolution number 63: 'On the supposition that there never was to be but one individual in the world at any one time who was properly a complete Christian.'[12] He reasoned that at any one moment in time, there must be one man alive who is regarded by God to be the most complete Christian in his day. Edwards purposed to be this man. With this lofty goal fixed squarely in his gaze, he continued: 'Resolved: I will act just as I would do if I strove with all of my might to be that one who should live in my time.'[13] It was by no accident that this nineteen-year-old young man, serving at the time as an intern pastor on Wall Street in downtown New York, would become America's foremost pastor, preacher, philosopher, theologian, and author.

As a teenage boy, Edwards set a course for his life that he would glorify God by striving to be the most complete Christian in his generation. On January 12, 1723, Jonathan Edwards wrote in his diary the following:

> I have been before God, and have given myself, all that I am and have, to God; so that I am not, in any respect, my own. I can challenge no right [to] this understanding, this will, these affections, which are in me. Neither have I any right to this body, or any of its members – no right to this tongue, these hands, these feet; no right to these senses, these eyes, these ears, this smell, or this taste. I have given myself clear away, and have not retained any thing as my own. I have been this morning to Him, and told Him, that I gave myself wholly to Him. I have this morning told Him that I did take Him for my whole portion, looking on nothing else as any part of my happiness, nor acting as if it were; and His law, for the constant rule of my obedience; and would fight with all my might against the world, the flesh, and the devil, to the

---

12. Jonathan Edwards, *The Works of Jonathan Edwards*, Vol. 1 (Banner of Truth Trust, 1998), 22.

13. ibid.

end of my life; and that I did believe in Jesus Christ, and did receive Him as a Prince and Saviour; and that I would adhere to the faith and obedience of the gospel, however hazardous and difficult the confession and practice of it may be. Now, henceforth, I am not to act, in any respect as my own.[14]

It is clear by this diary entry that young Edwards purposed to live a holy life. The high truths of the doctrines of grace had been translated into personal holiness in his soul. So these truths must transform our lives into our growth in godliness.

This is the spirit of what Peter challenged the Christians of his day. The apostle called them – and you and me – to conduct ourselves in fear during our whole time on the earth (1:17). He calls us to purify our souls (1:22) by putting aside all sins (2:1). He urges us to long for the pure milk of the Word (2:2) so that we may grow in respect to our salvation (2:3). He calls us to keep our behavior excellent (2:12) by following in the steps of Christ (2:21). He calls us to live with chaste and respectful behavior (3:2) by sanctifying Christ in our hearts (3:15). He calls us to humble ourselves (5:4-5) with a sober spirit (5:8). He calls us to resist the devil firm in our faith (5:8-9), seeking someone to devour (5:6).

May God grant much sanctifying grace to this exciting awakening known as New Calvinism. May He mature and reform the lives of all who are Young, Restless, and Reformed. And may they live radically separated lives.

---

14. ibid., 25.

4

Spirit Empowered?

Conrad Mbewe

HE issue of power in Christian living and ministry is one that cannot be overlooked by a true believer. This is, first of all, because we have an ongoing fight against indwelling or remaining sin in our lives. The fight is real. We want to overcome the enemy within. It keeps us from being the kind of people we know we ought to be. We fall short of loving God with all our hearts, minds, souls, and strength, and loving our neighbors as we love ourselves. It also causes us to often sin against God. We all identify with the cry of the apostle Paul in Romans 7 when he writes, 'So I find it to be a law that when I want to do right, evil lies close at hand. For I delight in the law of God, in my inner being, but I see in my members another law waging war against the law of my mind and making me captive to the law of sin that dwells in my members. Wretched man that I am! Who will deliver me from this body of death?' (Rom. 7:21-24 ESV). This causes us to want power. We want to be able to overcome this enemy within.

Another reason why we cannot overlook the subject of power in the Christian life and ministry is because if we are truly regenerate we not only want to serve the Lord but we also want to serve Him effectively and fruitfully. We want our evangelistic work to be fruitful so that through us God will bring people to Himself in repentance and faith. We also want our lives to have a positive spiritual impact upon fellow Christians so that they might be built up in the faith through our ministry to them. We have a Master to serve and we would like to end our lives saying with the apostle Paul, 'I have fought the good fight, I have finished the race, I have kept the faith. Henceforth there is laid up for me the crown of righteousness, which the Lord, the righteous judge, will award to me on that Day' (2 Tim. 4:7-8 esv).

Those of us who are preachers wish we could say as Charles Haddon Spurgeon said:

> As a church we have lived in revivals for nearly twenty years. There has never been a time that I can remember when there have not been souls converted in our midst. I do not know that there has ever been a Sabbath without a conversion in this place. I do not think there has been a sermon without a conversion.[1]

We long for a day when we can speak like this.

For these two reasons, therefore, we seek to be empowered. For the purpose of this chapter, we will concentrate on the second reason – empowerment for service.

The Biblical Answer to this Cry

Our reading of the Scriptures points us to the fact that this empowerment that we seek is by the Holy Spirit whom God

---

1. Metropolitan Tabernacle Pulpit, vol. 55, pg. 143.

has given to us. To begin with, this is inseparably linked to the indwelling and sanctifying work of the Holy Spirit. He has one major agenda in our lives: to conform us to the likeness of Christ for the glory of God. In conforming us to the image of Christ in a practical way, He enables us to do the will of God from the heart. He strengthens us with a strength that is not our own so that we can say with the apostle Paul, 'I can do all things through him who strengthens me' (Phil. 4:13 ESV). Yet, because we are conscious that this is not our strength but that of God Himself, it keeps us humble and ever dependent on Him. As the apostle Paul once said, 'By the grace of God I am what I am, and his grace toward me was not in vain. On the contrary, I worked harder than any of them, though it was not I, but the grace of God that is with me' (1 Cor. 15:10 ESV).

Answered Through Spiritual Gifts

With respect to fruitfulness in Christian service, the Holy Spirit does so, first of all, by giving us gifts and abilities at the point of our conversion. That is the whole argument of 1 Corinthians 12. This is not something we seek for ourselves or ask from God but is given to us by the sovereign work of the Spirit. The NIV says, 'Now to each one, the manifestation of the Spirit is given for the common good… All these are the work of one and the same Spirit and he gives them to each one *just as he determines*' (1 Cor. 12:7, 11, emphasis mine).

Our role is not that of asking for a particular gift but that of using the gifts that are already given us by the Holy Spirit. Thus the apostle Paul would say, 'Having gifts that differ according to the grace given to us, let us use them: if prophecy, in proportion to our faith; if service, in our serving; the one who teaches, in his teaching; the one who exhorts, in his exhortation; the one who contributes, in generosity; the one who leads, with zeal; the one who does acts of mercy, with cheerfulness' (Rom. 12:6-8 esv). Paul takes it for granted that as long as we are part of the body of Christ we have gifts that the Holy Spirit has given us according to His grace. Therefore His appeal is: Let us use them!

In many ways, that is half of empowerment already – the Holy Spirit's enabling that causes us to enjoy doing what others fail to do. Sadly, we often underrate this in our quest for the extraordinary. Your ability to exegete Scripture and present it to others in such a way that both the giraffes and the lambs in the congregation are able to understand and go home edified is a gift of the Holy Spirit. He has empowered us to minister to His body. So, instead of seeking for what we do not have, we should be grateful for what we have and put it to good use. God knows what He wants to accomplish through us and He chose the right gifting for us so that He could do just that though our lives.

Answered by Making Us Effectual

There is a second way in which the Holy Spirit empowers us for service. It is in terms of Him making us spiritually effective in overcoming sin and rebellion towards God in the hearts of those to whom we minister. Surely, this is what the apostle Paul had in mind when he wrote:

> And I, when I came to you, brothers, did not come proclaiming to you the testimony of God with lofty speech or wisdom. For I decided to know nothing among you except Jesus Christ and him crucified. And I was with you in weakness and in fear and much trembling, and my speech and my message were not in plausible words of wisdom, but in demonstration of the Spirit and of power, so that your faith might not rest in the wisdom of men but in the power of God (1 Cor. 2:1-5 esv).

Paul was not merely referring to His gifting. He was referring to something that the Holy Spirit was doing with His gifting to break the power of sin in the lives of His listeners, even as they listened to Him. The apostle Paul also referred to this phenomenon when he wrote to the Thessalonians. He wrote, 'For we know, brothers loved by God, that he has chosen you, because our gospel came to you not only in word, but also in power and in the Holy Spirit and with full conviction' (1 Thess. 1:4-5 ESV). It was not only 'in word' but also 'in power'. Often, this is what we are really talking about when we speak about the Spirit's empowerment. This is what we want to experience as we minister to the lost and to God's people.

Charles Haddon Spurgeon once said:

> Unless the Holy Ghost blesses the Word, we who preach the gospel are of all men most miserable, for we have attempted a task that is impossible. We have entered on a sphere where nothing but the supernatural will ever avail. If the Holy Spirit does not renew the hearts of our hearers, we cannot do it. If the Holy Ghost does not regenerate them, we cannot. If he does not send the truth home into their souls, we might as well speak into the ear of a corpse.[2]

So, the question we all have on our minds is, how can we know this empowerment?

The answer is divided into two segments – God's sovereignty and human responsibility. The two must be kept in tandem.

God's Sovereignty in Election

Let us handle the first… God's sovereignty. With respect to our effectiveness in the lives of those who listen to us, sometimes

---

2. Metropolitan Tabernacle Pulpit, vol. 42, pg. 236.

God hardens human hearts and softens them to fulfill His own eternal purpose. It is totally beyond our scope, though God chooses to use us as instruments in His hands. That was certainly the case with Paul in Thessalonica. He wrote that he knew the Thessalonian brothers and sisters were loved by God and chosen by Him before time began. He was persuaded about this because when he went to preach among them his gospel was only 'in words' to the other people in Thessalonica who were hearing Paul but to these specific individuals it came 'not only in word but also in power and in the Holy Spirit and with full conviction' (1 Thess. 1:5 ESV). This was not in fulfillment of a formula that Paul had that resulted in powerful results. Rather, it was in fulfillment of a plan God made before He even created the world. It was the time He had designated to bring His elect into the kingdom and He was now fulfilling it through Paul. Thus He empowered him in an unusual way in the hearts of these specific individuals.

A hymn-writer captures this very well and says:

> I know not how the Spirit moves
> Convincing men of sin
> Revealing Jesus through the Word
> Creating faith in Him.
>
> (DANIEL WEBSTER WHITTLE, 1883)

Human Responsibility

Then there is the second part, which is human responsibility. Here is where our role is. We are to seek God's blessing upon our individual ministries through (1) godly living and (2) godly praying. This is what separates one servant of God from another in terms of being Spirit empowered. To begin with, in an ongoing way, God only uses holy instruments. The apostle Paul, writing to Timothy, said:

Now in a great house there are not only vessels of gold and silver but also of wood and clay, some for honorable use, some for dishonorable. Therefore, if anyone cleanses himself from what is dishonorable, he will be a vessel for honorable use, set apart as holy, useful to the master of the house, ready for every good work' (2 Tim. 2:20-21 ESV).

Spirit empowerment must never be divorced from personal holiness. Sadly, this is the fallacy of many leaders in the Charismatic movement who have brought the whole movement into disrepute. While making a lot of noise about how powerfully God is using them, some nosy journalists have unearthed scandals in their lives that would make your hair stand on end. Sometimes, it is their wives who have said, 'Enough is enough,' and opened the cupboards allowing the skeletons to fall out in full view of the watching world. That is not Spirit empowerment but mere showmanship. God uses holy instruments. As Robert Murray M'Cheyne once said, 'A holy minister is an awful weapon in the hands of God.'

Coupled with this hunger for godliness that is realized through a person cleansing himself from all that is sinful, there must be the desire to be used powerfully by God that expresses itself through actual prayers asking God to bless our labors. The apostle Paul once exhorted the Thessalonians, among whom he had known a real bumper harvest, saying, 'Finally, brothers, pray for us, that the word of the Lord may speed ahead and be honored, as happened among you' (2 Thess. 3:1 ESV). By saying, 'as happened among you,' Paul is referring to powerful conversions that took place in Thessalonica when he preached there. He wanted to see similar fruit where he currently was. He knew that God could grant this in answer to prayer and so he pleaded that they join him in praying for such results.

We may have never experienced the kind of revival that Paul had in Thessalonica or that Charles Haddon Spurgeon was speaking about in the sermon quoted earlier, but surely we should have a longing to see more fruit from our labors. This will be especially the case when we read church history and biographies and thus get to know the great works of Christ in other generations and in the lives of other ministers of the gospel. This will cause us to cry to God that He may use us powerfully by His Spirit. It will also cause us to ask others to pray for us that we may be unusually empowered by God's Spirit.

Up to this point we are on safe ground. Things get a little messy after this.

The Historic Reformed Position

The difficulty often arises when we go to narrative texts like the book of Acts and find passages in the Bible that suggest a post-conversion empowering, which sets you into a class of your own, e.g. 'You will receive power when the Holy Spirit has come upon you, and you will be my witnesses in Jerusalem and in all Judea and Samaria, and to the end of the earth' (Acts 1:8 ESV). Sure enough, Luke records, 'And with great power the apostles were giving their testimony to the resurrection of the Lord Jesus, and great grace was upon them all' (Acts 4:33 ESV). How are we to understand this? It has been a wrong understanding of texts such as these that has led many on the wrong path.

The historic Reformed position has been that we do not need our own individual 'Pentecosts'. We receive the Holy Spirit at the point of our conversion and consequently we do not need to ask God for the kind of experience that the apostles had on the day of Pentecost. As the apostles themselves later testified, 'We are witnesses to these things, and so is the Holy Spirit, whom God has given to those who obey him' (Acts 5:32 ESV). So, there is no receiving of the Holy Spirit again. Rather, what we need is to yield ourselves more and more to the work of the Holy Spirit in our lives, i.e. to be filled with the Holy Spirit.

Again, the historic Reformed position took it for granted that the extraordinary gifts of the Holy Spirit – such as speaking in tongues, interpretation of tongues, miraculous healing, etc. – had ceased with the passing on of the apostles in Bible times. Notice that this does not mean God cannot do something extraordinary or miraculous, especially in answer to the prayers of God's people. He is God! He can do all things. Nothing is impossible with God. Rather, this refers to the cessation of the *gifts* being embodied in individuals so that they are empowered to do the extraordinary in an ongoing way, as was the case with the apostles. So, any seeking of spiritual empowerment that suggests the restoration of such *gifts* must be biblically misinformed.

John Calvin wrote:

> The gift of healing, like the rest of the miracles, which the Lord willed to be brought forth for a time, has vanished away in order to make the preaching of the Gospel marvelous for ever.[3]

Martin Luther wrote:

> In the early Church the Holy Spirit was sent forth in visible form.... This visible outpouring of the Holy Spirit was necessary to the establishment of the early Church, as were also the miracles that accompanied the gift of the Holy Ghost.... Once the Church had been established and properly advertised by these miracles, the visible appearance of the Holy Ghost ceased.[4]

---

3. Institutes of Christian Religion, IV:19,18.
4. Commentary on Galatians 4, on chapter 4:6.

One hundred years later, during the Puritan era, *The 1689 London Baptist Confession of Faith* states towards the end of its very first paragraph:

> Therefore it pleased the Lord at sundry times and in divers manners to reveal Himself, and to declare that His will unto His church; and afterward for the better preserving and propagating of the truth, and for the more sure establishment and comfort of the church against the corruption of the flesh, and the malice of Satan, and of the world, to commit the same wholly unto writing; which maketh the Holy Scriptures to be most necessary, those former ways of God's revealing His will unto His people being now ceased.

This follows the rendering of *The Westminster Confession of Faith* of 1646 of the Presbyterian church and *The Savoy Declaration* of 1658 of the Congregational church. Between these three confessions of faith you have covered quite a large chunk of the main Reformed denominations in the Puritan era. It is evident that they all took the same position that the extraordinary revelatory gifts had ceased. We are safe to assume that this was the historic Reformed position. I will not try to prove the correctness of this position here. That is well treated elsewhere.

The New Continuationism

However, in the recent past there has been a resurgence of Calvinism that has caused this historic position to be held in question. It would be wrong to totally equate it to what has come to be called 'New Calvinism' because those who are often categorized as such are not homogenous in their beliefs concerning the miraculous gifts of the Holy Spirit. Many of them would also prefer to be called Continuationists (a very new term) rather than Charismatics as they seek to define themselves as not being Cessationists.

These terms can be quite confusing to a newcomer especially because they do not necessarily mean that everyone in one category believes the same things even with respect to the person and work of the Holy Spirit. Allowing for that, Continuationists are best seen as being on one end of the Charismatic spectrum and would largely differ primarily in practice with other conservative evangelical Charismatics. Then on the opposite end of the Charismatic spectrum – way, way over there – would be the likes of Benn Hinn and Creflo Dollar who have pushed the Charismatic agenda to such unbiblical limits that even their fellow Charismatics want nothing to do with them. In Africa, we have this latter brand becoming syncretistic with African Traditional Religions. It is beyond my assignment to help my reader work through the maze of the entire Charismatic spectrum.

Continuationists, like Charismatics, believe that the extraordinary gifts of the Holy Spirit that we read about in the book of Acts and some of the epistles (especially the book of 1 Corinthians) have continued to the present day. Preachers in Bible times were spiritually empowered in a most supernatural way and so should it be for us today. They argue that there is no obvious teaching in the Bible that such gifts would cease.

It should not surprise us that there should be such a revision within Reformed circles on the issue of spiritual gifts. We are now living more than one hundred years after the Asuza Street revival in California that led to the birth of the Pentecostal and Charismatic movements. This movement has had tremendous impact upon Christian doctrine and practice, especially around the issues of worship and of empowerment for Christian service. Old boundaries have been questioned and in many denominations have even been moved. In the light of the many claims to healings and miracles, one can no longer take it for granted that the extraordinary gifts of the Holy Spirit ceased with the passing on of the apostles. Many individuals with a Calvinistic Reformed position have taken on a Continuationist, if not Charismatic, position.

There has also been a reaction against the dead but orthodox preaching that has characterized much of Reformed preaching, especially in the mainline churches around the world. Doctrinally, such preaching cannot be faulted. Yet, there are hardly any conversions being seen and the churches are either dying or stagnant. It is partly a reaction to this – in contrast to the growth and excitement in Pentecostal and Charismatic circles – that has caused many to peep across the fence to see if there is something that most of today's Reformed preaching could be missing. The conclusion has been that such preaching has the Word but lacks the Spirit's empowerment. How else can one explain the growth of the Pentecostal and Charismatic churches across the road from the stunted nature of neighboring Reformed churches where biblical truth continues to be taught?

As I seek to comment on this, it needs to be stated from the onset that any effort at addressing our spiritual deficiency should always be a most welcome move. Therefore, the very fact that many Calvinistic churches and church leaders are raising the question of 'power' (or at least the lack of it) must be a source of great encouragement. It should lead to greater humility and prayer to God for His help. This can only be for the good of the church. So, as I address some of the areas of great concern, we must not lose sight of the good that this self-searching is doing. We must not throw out the baby with the bathwater.

Thankfully, we are now at a point in history where we can look back and judge whether this capitulation of the orthodox historic position on the cessation of the charismata has been helpful or not. Has the opening up of the door to the seeking of the extraordinary gifts within Calvinistic Reformed circles brought about the Spirit empowerment that was being looked for or has it resulted in a loss rather than a gain? I think that with the benefit of hindsight, an honest appraisal must show that it is a loss. Here are a few areas that are worth chewing over as possible causes for concern. Notice the downgrade.

Proof from the Book of Acts

We are allowing an interpretation of the book of Acts that has long been agreed on as wrong. This is because the view that there is such a post-Pentecostal experience of being 'endued with power from on high' (to borrow a phrase that was once a catch-phrase) is not sustainable from the didactic Scriptures. Most people who seek to propagate this view, therefore, tend to go to the book of Acts for their support. Yet, it is an established fact that the effort to develop doctrine out of the book of Acts has always been fraught with exegetical and historical difficulties. It has been well said that you do not go to historical passages in Scripture to establish doctrine but rather to illustrate it. This is because a lot of what happens at any one point in God's redemptive plan tends to be for that time in history. We are relenting on this well-established principle. This inevitably will have far-reaching ramifications because if we allow it in this case, how shall we deny it to others who will want to use the book of Acts to allow for choosing church officers by casting lots, baptizing only in Jesus' name, and going to Jerusalem to resolve doctrinal issues.

The Silence in the Epistles

It is unlike Reformed Christians to fail to see the elephant in the room. When one goes to the epistles, and especially the Pastoral Epistles, the silence about a one-off 'formula' for spiritual power in Christian service is ear piercing! Surely, should this not be instructive? If what we all needed as preachers in order to bring down the strongholds of Satan in the hearts of people were some fresh 'enduement of power from on high' would Paul not have mentioned it to Timothy and Titus in his epistles to them? After all, they would have been crying for more fruit to their ministries as we all do today. Paul would have given them the answer once and for all, and it would have been there waiting for all of us to read about.

Once we justify this form of swallowing a camel (the silence in the Epistles) while straining a gnat (some apparent proof in Acts), we lose the balance of the true Christian life that is painted by the sum-total of biblical revelation. It is a matter of time before this touches other areas of Christian living. Our approach should always be to go to the Bible and allow it to give us the answers to the questions we are posing today. Where we find silence, let us realize that perhaps our perceived answer may be wrong.

The Loss of Exegetical Acumen

The slide to the next level soon becomes apparent. In seeking to argue for the continuation of the extraordinary gifts of the Spirit, there has been a failure to interpret Scripture using the well-worn hermeneutical principles that have been a safeguard for evangelical and conservative Christianity for ages such as the maintenance of the context of a text.

Let me use one example. I heard one leading Continuationist (whom I have a lot of respect for and whose shoes I am unworthy to untie) say that he was still asking God to give him the gift of tongues based on the text, 'Earnestly desire the higher gifts...' (1 Cor. 12:31 ESV). Simply asking the doctrinal question, 'Does God give us spiritual gifts at the point of our conversion or does He give them to us in answer to our prayers later in life?' should put this matter behind us. The chapter itself teaches that the Spirit of God gives His gifts to His people in absolute sovereignty: 'All these are empowered by one and the same Spirit, who apportions to each one individually *as he wills*' (1 Cor. 12:11 ESV, emphasis mine). We have already talked about that.

However, my concern is greater than that. The context of the text is not about individuals being encouraged to pray to God to give them one gift or another. Far from it! It is about the church as a body allowing more (and in that sense 'desiring') *the use of* the gifts that edify the wider body rather than gifts that tend only towards the personal edification of the person with the gift. That is so obvious from the context.

It is disconcerting when Reformed Christian pastors and scholars start losing their exegetical acumen like this. And one wonders why this is almost exclusively when they are trying to somehow show that the extraordinary gifts of the Holy Spirit are supposed to be in full use in the Christian church today. In other areas their acumen still seems to be intact. This is worrying and cannot be a gain. It must be a loss.

A Door that has been Opened

While the leading proponents of the Continuationist position are still alive among us, I do not think we are going to see their followers plunge further down the precipice. However, as long as the obvious contradiction is not addressed, and exegetical principles are not restored, I would not be surprised if the next generation gives to us the kind of oxymoron that we are now seeing in evangelical circles back home in Africa. Let me explain.

From where I stand as a Reformed Baptist pastor ministering in Africa, perhaps my greatest concern has been the door that is opened to Charismatic excesses by the very people that ought to keep that door closed. The Continuationist position gives legitimacy to the Charismatic movement by becoming nothing more than a shade less than the full-blown position. Follow the logic and before you know it you can see how the current Charismatic chaos cannot be arrested once a door is opened to the post nineteenth century understanding of miraculous gifts today, which is in vogue in Pentecostal circles.

It all begins with the position that we need God's power restored in the church through amazing feats, including the restoration of the revelatory gifts. God must still speak to His church through extraordinary revelations. The Bible is not enough. Once that is accepted, the place that the written Word of God is supposed to have in the life of believers and in the life of the church is inevitably compromised. It is degraded and people start preferring that which is out of the ordinary. Then we also want to see those acts of power in terms of people being healed and delivered every time the church meets.

In Bible times, there were actual apostles who had the authority from God to be physically present to correct what was going wrong and especially wrong teaching that was being spread in the name of Christ. Today, even when we speak about men with 'apostolic' ministries, we know that it is only the extreme Charismatics who dare to call themselves 'apostles'. They do not tell us who appointed them to that role and they carry no authority beyond that which they usurp from the local churches that they oversee. Without such truly authoritative figures – since the apostles have all passed on – by what authority do you silence the many gainsayers that have invaded the church since this door was opened?

With no apostles to authoritatively state God's position and the Bible degraded from its position of unequalled sway, the door is now open for the most bizarre to happen in the church. This is what is happening in the church in Africa. Sadly, in our quest for Spirit empowerment, we may have inadvertently lent a hand to this instead of helping to nip it in the bud.

In Conclusion

Let me say as I close that I do not doubt both the spirituality and the integrity of those whom I personally know and admire who have taken up the Continuationist position within what has now come to be called New Calvinism. I have the greatest respect for them. I also think that their concern to see more life and heat among Reformed brethren especially within the mainline churches ought to be commended. There is nothing as off-putting as someone speaking about 'amazing grace' as if he is sitting on a cube of ice.

I also think we should be grateful for the fact that New Calvinism has managed to bring the doctrines of grace before the watching world in a way that was previously not happening. The light was too long hidden under the bushels of sixteenth and seventeenth century tombs and tightly concealed within the walls of our twentieth century Bible colleges and seminaries. To see it being passionately debated and glowingly embraced by a new generation of young people to the level that it has should warm the hearts of all true servants of God. It speaks well for the future of the church because a church's doctrinal strength is the foundation on which it builds all its works of evangelism and edification.

However, I also plead that the New Calvinists should remain firmly rooted in the Scriptures especially as they seek spiritual empowerment. The biblical teaching on how to be spiritually empowered is clear. Capitulating to the Pentecostal and Charismatic understanding of this will not be a gain but a loss primarily because that understanding is not Scriptural. Calvinism has been about *sola Scriptura* above all things. We dare not throw that away because the moment we do that we would have lost the battle for the truth altogether.

5

A Call for Discernment

Tim Challies

✣

IT is too early to confidently predict how history will regard New Calvinism. It is possible that it may be only the smallest footnote in the long and storied history of the Christian faith. It is equally possible, though, that it will be viewed as a significant chapter in which God used very ordinary people to accomplish His extraordinary work. In my contribution to this book I focus on the future of New Calvinism. If New Calvinism is to have a sweeping impact that will last for years to come, what strengths must it continue to build and to emphasize? What sinful temptations must it avoid?

To answer such questions we first need to consider the nature and history of New Calvinism. Is it a trend? Is it a movement? Is it organic or planned? Is it merely a money-making scheme for publishers or an influence-creating scheme for ministries and their leaders? And from where did it arise in the first place?

In many ways New Calvinism had its genesis as a response to the church growth movement, which, heading into the new millennium, was a dominant force within Evangelicalism. Leaders like Rick Warren and Bill Hybels were writing books and leading conferences that advocated a form of Christian pragmatism. Church leaders were told that if they followed the programs and mimicked the successes of megachurches they, too, could see wild growth. This led to a programmatic, big-box Christianity that could be bought and sold, transferred and duplicated. *The Purpose Driven Church*, the manual for the pastor, spawned *The Purpose Driven Life* as the manual for the individual. Sermons became short and topical instead of long and expositional, pastoral prayer was removed from worship services in favor of prayers of response and commitment, the old hymns were neglected in favor of new choruses, doctrine was displaced by felt needs.

A growing number of people began to express concern with this movement and they responded in at least two very different ways. One group determined that they would focus on recovering authentic Christian *community* and began to refer to themselves as the Emerging Church. They called for a new kind of Christianity that downplayed theological distinctions in favor of authenticity and community. They met in small, local gatherings and fostered online communities. But theologically they soon drifted back to the familiar liberalism of the early twentieth century. The authenticity they advocated too often came at the expense of the theology the Bible demands. Without robust theological grounding and without sound institutions the movement quickly drifted, then faded.

The second group determined that they would look back to the theology of the Reformers and recover authentic Christian *doctrine*. They called for the recovery of doctrine that had been forgotten, neglected, or displaced – doctrine known as Calvinism or Reformed theology. They began to gather around a handful of notable Calvinist preachers with John MacArthur, John Piper, and R.C. Sproul most notable among them. Soon they began to gather in conferences like Together for the Gospel while organizations like The Gospel Coalition began to define and organize the movement. A new generation of leaders rose up, led by men like Albert Mohler, Mark Dever, C. J. Mahaney and behind them the next generation – Kevin DeYoung, Matt Chandler, and David Platt among them. Christian publishers turned their attention to the movement, releasing hundreds, then thousands of books by and for this group. Christian and mainstream publications described and defined the movement with monickers such as *Young, Restless, Reformed* and *the New Calvinism*. Josh aptly defined it for us in his opening chapter saying:

> New Calvinism as a movement can be defined as an eclectic and at times edgy group of multi-ethnic, multi-denominational, and age-diverse Reformed people from all parts of the world who are hungry for a big sovereign God. These people are Christ-exalting, Spirit-driven, missions-motivated, and Bible-believing Christians who are seeking to know God, worship God, serve God, and bring glory to God.

New Calvinism began as an organic movement and grew by connections made through the Internet and, in particular, through the new medium of social media. Social media led people to books, to podcasts, to sermon archives, to conferences, to churches. At its best, this New Calvinism is an organic, worldwide movement of Christians who long to know and serve God. But New Calvinism is also a relatively new movement and one that is dominated by young people. It is an untested movement that has not yet been challenged by 'the next big thing.' It is in many ways an undefined movement that continues to negotiate its boundaries to determine who and what is in and who and what is out. It is an increasingly diverse movement that spans the globe, yet whose most prominent personalities are predominantly middle-aged, Caucasian, American men.

In what follows I will first identify God's grace within New Calvinism, offering six notable strengths of the movement. I will follow this by suggesting six potential weaknesses the movement would do well to address.

Identifying Grace

Whatever else we can say about New Calvinism we can say this: It displays many, many evidences of God's grace. It is beyond dispute that God has been blessing His people and glorifying His name through this movement.

Enthusiasm for Sound Doctrine

If there is an unofficial textbook for New Calvinism it has to be Wayne Grudem's *Systematic Theology*. If there is an unofficial study Bible the honor has to go to the enormous *ESV Study Bible*. The movement's elder statesmen are pastor-theologians and its rising generation of leaders are primarily preachers. Its favored mode of communication is the expository sermon and its conferences are based primarily around hour-long expositions of Scripture. Its books, whether for children or adults, whether for new believers or seasoned saints, are committed to displaying the centrality of the gospel and to promoting the glory of God in all things. Its radio programs and podcasts are led by men and women who teach the Bible and, through the Bible, the uncompromised truths of the Christian faith. Even its music is deliberately theological, helping generate a revival of hymnody. From stem to stern, New Calvinism is a movement founded upon and defined by its doctrine.

In many ways the movement arose as a response to the inadequate teaching of churches caught up in the tenets of church growth. People came to a saving knowledge of Christ, but soon found themselves starving, longing to be fed by and from the Word of God. They were unsatisfied with the paltry diet of 'sermonettes for Christianettes' and went looking for churches and ministries that could satisfy their spiritual cravings. Inevitably they went online and there they navigated to the books, blogs, podcasts, and preachers of New Calvinism. A few Google searches led them to like-minded churches where they would be fed the pure milk of the Word (1 Pet. 2:2).

This enthusiasm for sound doctrine is a mark of God's favor and blessing. The inadequacy of the church growth movement is directly related to its inadequate theology and the failure of the Emerging Church was inevitable because of its failure to embrace sound doctrine. New Calvinism, though, is built upon the firm foundation of the historic doctrine of the Christian faith. God has awakened people who for too long have been content with poor theology and I am convinced that He will now use these awakened Christians to approach the world with missionary fervor.

Local-Church Centrality

It would be easy to define New Calvinism by its many conferences. From John MacArthur's Shepherds' Conference, to John Piper's Bethlehem Conference for Pastors, to Alistair Begg's The Basics Conference, not to mention The Gospel Coalition and Together for the Gospel with their biannual events, New Calvinism is a movement made up of many conferences. It would also be easy to define New Calvinism by its many ministries and organizations: John MacArthur's Grace To You, John Piper's Desiring God, R. C. Sproul's

Ligonier Ministries, and again, The Gospel Coalition and Together for the Gospel. Yet to define the movement by any of those ministries would be to miss the point because New Calvinism is first a movement of Christians within their local churches.

One of the most important marks of New Calvinism is its focus on the centrality of the local church and its emphasis on healthy local churches. Each of these conferences and each of these organizations is committed to strengthening the local church either through teaching and encouraging its pastors or by providing material and resources that will serve the congregation. Each of them is committed to avoiding interference with the local church by emphasizing the importance of congregational and denominational authority and autonomy. This is an appropriate emphasis because God's plan for the world is not conferences or ministries but strong, Bible-based, local churches led by qualified leaders. New Calvinism gains strength by these conferences and ministries, but does its most important work through tens of thousands of local churches.

Biblical Ecumenism

It is a tragic reality of life in a fallen world that we find it far easier to splinter than to unite. And, indeed, much of church history can be told by the divisions that have kept Christian from Christian. Some of these divisions have been necessary to protect the purity of Christ's church, but too many have been unnecessary, petty disputes over the finest theological nuances.

From its inception, New Calvinism has been a movement that has emphasized a biblical ecumenism. United on the gospel and on a few key implications of the gospel, the movement has sought to unite Christians in shared relationship, ministry, and mission so that Presbyterians and Baptists gladly exchange pulpits united together on the gospel. This spirit of unity has fostered relationships locally and globally, leading to The Gospel Coalition with its international scope but also to a host of independent chapters intent on building gospel relationships across particular regions or nations. Together for the Gospel draws great crowds to Louisville every two years but has spawned hundreds of similar local and regional events. Such groups are diverse by their design, drawing together denominations, churches, and individuals that might otherwise prefer to remain independent and unaffiliated.

This ecumenism exists because the gospel has taken root. The main thing has remained the main thing and Christians have been willing to subordinate the disputable matters to those that are beyond dispute. This ecumenism has given hope to those who despaired at the church's tendency to divide and it has brought the joy of seeing how others understand and express their deeply-held theological convictions. It has pushed every person to better evaluate what can unite us and what must not be allowed to divide us.

International Impact

New Calvinism began primarily in America, was given its names by American publications, is led primarily by Americans, and is dominated by American Christians. Despite all of this, it is and always has been an international movement that is making its mark all around the globe. Its books are shipped around the world and its blogs accessed from every country on earth. Major conferences may draw attendees from forty, fifty, or even more nations. Wherever there are Christians and wherever those Christians are eager to be taught and trained, there are people who associate themselves with this movement. It is increasingly a truly international movement.

New Calvinism is also growing in its mission reach. While it was formed around certain theological distinctions, those doctrinal underpinnings have always demanded that its adherents express their theology in mission. John Piper, David Platt, Paul Washer and others like them have emphasized the responsibility of all Christians to serve and support global missions. Churches, denominations and sending agencies associated with New Calvinism have been faithful to send missionaries across the world and also to create excellent resources to serve them there.

Deploying New Technologies

Even a brief survey of church history shows that worldwide Christian movements have often followed close on the heels of new technologies. In the book of Acts we learn that first-century persecution scattered the first Christians all across the known world. This was made possible largely through the recent technology of the Roman roads. The Romans had laid roads to transport armies and carry trade from one end of their empire to the other, and the same roads that carried the feet of soldiers and merchants soon also carried the feet of missionaries. Fifteen centuries later the new technology of the printing press provided the means of distribution for the writings of the Reformers and, even more so, for the new translations of God's Word, the Bible. These are just two of many examples and in both of them it is difficult to imagine the glorious result without the recent technological innovation.

Today we are witnessing the dawn of the digital revolution. In just a short time we have experienced the advent of a host of new tools and all the capabilities they bring. It must not be lost on us that most of these tools exist for going and communicating – the very tasks God calls us to in the Great Commission. Never in all of human history have people been as accessible as they are today. Never before have we been able to have people and words go so far so fast.

New Calvinism has been on the front lines of creating, adapting, and using these new tools. Web sites, blogs, conference live-streaming, podcasts, YouTube, digital books and Bibles – though none of these existed even a few short years ago, it is difficult to imagine New Calvinism without them. Each of them has been understood and harnessed for God's purposes.

Grounding in Church History

Every generation grapples with the temptation to discount or neglect their forbears, to assume they have little to learn from those who have gone before. New Calvinism, though, has been shaped by previous generations of Christians and by pastors and teachers who lived in centuries past. Thus a final strength of New Calvinism is its desire to orient itself within the long history of the Christian faith.

As much as New Calvinism has emphasized correct doctrine, it has also emphasized church history. It has already produced hundreds of biographies, most of them written for a general audience and many targeted squarely at children. Conferences often feature church historians who draw lessons from the subjects of their studies. There has been a revival of interest in the Puritans and new books are filled with as many quotes from the sixteenth century as from the twentieth or twenty-first. The Reformers are revered for all we owe to them for their work in rescuing and reviving the gospel from cold Catholicism. In this way New Calvinism looks back even as it looks forward, it seeks to draw wisdom from ancient sources even as it applies that wisdom to modern realities.

Conclusion

In these ways and so many more New Calvinism is displaying evidences that God's hand of blessing is upon it. Souls are being saved, lives are being transformed, churches are being strengthened, missionaries are being sent, the work the Lord has given us is being carried on.

Weaknesses to Avoid

New Calvinism displays many strengths, many evidences of the grace of God. Yet we do well to maintain a wary, cautious posture. Strengths can expose weaknesses, success can breed arrogance, good intentions can bring about bad effects. I would like to suggest a series of weaknesses New Calvinism must avoid.

The Danger of Trendiness

The first and perhaps most significant temptation that New Calvinism must avoid is the temptation of trendiness. There was a time when Reformed theology was considered a death knell to ministry, a time when few people held to Reformed theology, a time when few people who held to Reformed theology helmed churches or ministries that had a significant profile. Today, though, there are a host of much-admired multi-million dollar ministries and megachurches that are distinctly Reformed in their profession and expression of the Christian faith. Reformed authors are selling tens or hundreds of thousands of books and receiving awards for their work. Reformed seminaries are attracting students from around the world. This mainstreaming of New Calvinism could point to a permanent shift in Evangelicalism. But, more dangerously, it could point to the existence of a trend or a fad.

New Calvinism did not arise from within a void but as a form of protest against what was then considered 'mainstream Evangelicalism.' The church growth movement with all of its programs and its emphasis on seeker-friendliness had de-emphasized doctrine to such an extent that many Christians were starving for spiritual food. Many of these people began to support Reformed ministries and to migrate to Reformed churches. The trickle eventually became a deluge. But it is possible and perhaps even likely that some people have simply jumped from one fad to another. They made the leap from church growth to New Calvinism not because of deeply held convictions but because this is where the excitement was. They were swept up in a flood and are now along for the ride.

We will not know how many have simply followed a trend until the next thing comes along. It seems inevitable that at some point in the future Reformed theology will no longer be celebrated as it is today. Eventually books and conferences will insist that there is something newer, something better, something purer, and something with greater promise. At that time we will learn how many are trend-followers and how many really are committed to Reformed truth. Today is the time for individuals, churches, and ministries to ensure they truly are committed to biblical truth as it is defined by Reformed theology. Now is the time to firmly anchor themselves in the deepest bedrock of truth.

The Danger of Celebrityism

Another danger New Calvinism needs to face is the danger of celebrity and celebrityism. Any movement is led by leaders – it is obvious and unavoidable. Eventually, though, a movement needs to question the place of its leaders and consider what the movement would be without them. Just as New Calvinists need to consider whether they are simply following the latest, coolest trend, they also need to consider whether they are simply following today's trend-setters and today's exciting leaders.

New Calvinism has already committed a few significant gaffes in relation to celebrity, handing position and influence to church and ministry leaders who quickly proved themselves unworthy of it. Influence was given to those who achieved a certain level of fame or notoriety. Book sales and church size were mistaken as a sign of God's favor, and this caused too many people to overlook an alarming lack of godly character and qualification. Their eventual downfall caused grief and consternation to their followers – followers who should have seen it coming.

While mega-conferences surely point to a desire to hear good preaching and to be challenged and sharpened by biblical truth, they also point to a desire to hear celebrities preach and to be where the action is. Megachurch leaders have had to grapple with the fact that too many people join their churches because of its dynamic leader and not because of deeply held convictions or the desire to love and serve others.

It is good to honor those who have led well and whose godly convictions have shaped others. It is good to honor those who are worthy of imitation. But always we must first follow Christ for, as one old author reminds us, 'The best of men are but men at their best.'

The Danger of Pride

There are few dangers in the world greater than the danger of recognition. For many years Calvinism had little to fear from this danger because it was nearly invisible to the eyes of the wider Christian world and the culture around it. However, the growth of New Calvinism has brought with it recognition that this movement is growing and is exerting some influence on church and culture. With influence and recognition comes the temptation to pride.

This kind of pride may manifest itself in gleeful comparisons to those who are truly Christians but who hold to different theological convictions. It may manifest itself in looking down at those who attempt to lovingly critique the movement, pointing out its flaws and shortcomings. It may manifest itself in a failure to seriously self-assess the movement, its ministries, its emphases, and its leaders. Whatever the temptation, it will begin first within the hearts of people and then manifest itself in their thoughts, words, and actions.

New Calvinism will inevitably fade and fail if it allows itself to become self-congratulatory, if it somehow begins to think that God has used people because of who they are rather than despite who they are.

The Danger of Boundaries

Another danger that faces New Calvinism is the danger related to boundaries. As this movement grows it is facing unprecedented challenges in erecting and maintaining boundaries around the movement. Because there is no central government with authoritative jurisdiction over New Calvinism, these boundaries are being negotiated by the movement as a whole.

From its earliest days, New Calvinism gladly drew together Presbyterians and Baptists. As time has progressed it has expanded to Anglican and Dutch Reformed denominations and then to a host of independent churches and associations. New Calvinism has also welcomed Charismatics and Cessationists who align together on the centrality of the gospel and the validity of Reformed theology. This ecumenism has been a source of learning and encouragement for New Calvinists, so that even the very nature of Calvinism has had to be negotiated between those who insist a Calvinist must adhere to all five of the traditional five points of Calvinism and those who are content with four. It has been a source of learning and encouragement but has also been a source of challenge as to why others are excluded or exactly where the lines are drawn.

Varying beliefs on gender roles provides an interesting case study. New Calvinism has always been complementarian, insisting that God has made men and women to serve distinct, complementary roles within family and local church. In this way men are called to give leadership, especially through the teaching and preaching role in the church, and women are to joyfully follow that leadership. However, over time we have seen various challenges to the boundaries of complementarianism. Can a woman serve as a deacon within the church or is that a leadership role? Can a woman teach men at a conference or at a Bible study? Can a woman preach at a Sunday morning worship service if she does so under the clear authority of male elders? Complementarians continue to negotiate these boundaries.

A danger the New Calvinism faces is the danger of drawing boundaries too loosely, of endorsing beliefs that profess a point of theology but redraw it (as may be the case with a complementarian church that invites women to preach) or, conversely, of drawing boundaries too rigidly (as may be the case with a complementarian church that does not permit women to serve in any kind of teaching or leading role whatsoever). Any movement needs boundaries, but those boundaries must be drawn with wisdom and charity.

The Danger of Homogeneity

As human beings we tend to be most comfortable around those who are most similar to ourselves. It is for this reason that our church communities tend to drift toward uniformity rather than diversity and why we have such difficultly embracing variety. Over time, and without deliberate application of the gospel, churches will inevitably become less, not more, diverse until churches are made up almost entirely of people of one socio-economic background, one ethnicity, or even one view of disputable matters such as education. Movements are prone to the same temptation.

New Calvinism has largely been led, shaped, and defined by Caucasian, American, middle-class men. For that reason it inevitably has the flavor and the biases of Caucasian, American, middle-class men. Reformed conferences display very little diversity. A quick survey of four major events which between them will attract nearly 20,000 attendees show a combined total of thirty-eight keynote speakers. Of these thirty-eight speakers, two are African-American and one is from South America. All the others are white males, mostly from America but with three from the United Kingdom and Canada.

Despite this uniformity in conference speakers, the movement has diversified and is drawing in Christians of many nations, many ethnicities, many levels of richness and poverty. If the movement is to honor its many adherents and reach many more it will need to diversify its voices. Those with positions of prominence and leadership must eventually display the diversity of the movement. Those who have positions of prominence and leadership must joyfully and deliberately help raise up leaders within other demographics.

The Danger of Cold Theology

The final danger I wish to highlight is the danger of cold theology or what we might even term theological idolatry. Because New Calvinism is a movement defined by its theology and especially fond of its theology, there is a temptation to emphasize the theology instead of the God who gave it to us. There is a temptation to win people to a theological viewpoint rather than win them to Christ, to grow more enthusiastic about our theology than the gospel, to place more emphasis on defending what we believe than preaching the gospel that saves. There is a danger in confusing Calvinism with Christianity, the doctrines of grace with the gospel of grace. While we must tenaciously hold and even deepen our Reformed convictions, we must always acknowledge that the Christian world is wider than mere Calvinism. Even if Calvinism is the purest expression of biblical truth, it is not the only one. God does not call us to save people to Calvinism. No one has ever gone to heaven because they've properly understood predestination. They are saved when they put their faith in the Lord Jesus Christ and receive the benefits of what He accomplished for them on Calvary.

Always we must remember that Calvinism does not exist for itself but to magnify the glory of God and to win people to Christ. We should not want or need to be known for our Calvinism, but for our love, for our desire to do good to others and draw attention to the God who has saved us.

Conclusion

I began this chapter by saying it is too early to confidently predict how history will regard New Calvinism. This is true, but it is not too early for us to consider and determine together how that history will eventually be written. If New Calvinism is simply a trend, a movement, or a marketing machine then by all means, let's let it die. But if New Calvinism really does represent doctrine that the Bible makes plain, if it really does represent people who are committed to glorifying God by living for the good of others, then let's determine that we will rejoice in and press into the many evidences of God's grace, and let's determine that we will look for and address the potential weaknesses. Let's be relentless in our pursuit of God and His glory for the good of all the nations.

Christian Focus Publications

Our mission statement –

STAYING FAITHFUL
In dependence upon God we seek to impact the world through literature faithful to His infallible Word, the Bible. Our aim is to ensure that the Lord Jesus Christ is presented as the only hope to obtain forgiveness of sin, live a useful life and look forward to heaven with Him.

Our books are published in four imprints:

CHRISTIAN FOCUS

Popular works including biographies, commentaries, basic doctrine and Christian living.

CHRISTIAN HERITAGE

Books representing some of the best material from the rich heritage of the church.

MENTOR

Books written at a level suitable for Bible College and seminary students, pastors, and other serious readers. The imprint includes commentaries, doctrinal studies, examination of current issues and church history.

CF4•K

Children's books for quality Bible teaching and for all age groups: Sunday school curriculum, puzzle and activity books; personal and family devotional titles, biographies and inspirational stories – because you are never too young to know Jesus!

Christian Focus Publications Ltd,
Geanies House, Fearn, Ross-shire,
IV20 1TW, Scotland, United Kingdom.
www.christianfocus.com